VISUAL QUICKSTART GUIDE

OBJECTIVE-C

Steven Holzner

Peachpit Press

Visual QuickStart Guide

Objective-C

Steven Holzner

Peachpit Press

1249 Eighth Street
Berkeley, CA 94710
510/524-2178
510/524-2221 (fax)

Find us on the Web at www.peachpit.com.
To report errors, please send a note to errata@peachpit.com.
Peachpit Press is a division of Pearson Education.

Editor: Judy Ziajka
Production Coordinator: Myrna Vladic
Compositor: Deb Roberti
Proofreader: Wendy Sharp
Indexer: FireCrystal Communications
Cover Design: Peachpit Press

ISBN 13: 978-0-321-69946-6
ISBN 10: 0-321-69946-7

9 8 7 6 5 4 3 2 1

Printed and bound in the United States of America

Dedication

To Nancy, of course!

Acknowledgments

The book you hold in your hands is the product of many people's work. I would particularly like to thank Wendy Sharp and Judy Ziajka for their tireless efforts to make this book the best it can be and Danny Kalev for his careful technical review of the entire manuscript.

TABLE OF CONTENTS

Introduction

Welcome to Objective-C. This book is your guided tour of this exciting language, and it gives you what you need to start working with Objective-C at once.

Using Objective-C, you can write professional programs that make use of many object-oriented features—from the basics up to advanced class inheritance and exception (run-time error) handling.

Objective-C runs on many different platforms. For the most part, your code should work unchanged on all platforms that Objective-C supports, but where differences in support exist, this book points them out to you.

This book starts with the basics and continues on through advanced topics. You'll begin by looking at how to get Objective-C started and how to run basic programs. From there, you'll explore data handling, again starting with the basics and moving on through advanced topics.

After looking at how to write your own functions, you'll wrap functions and data together into objects—the core of Objective-C programming. And when you start working with object-oriented programming, the lid is off—and we'll push the envelope as far as it can go.

That's the plan, then: to present a guided tour of Objective-C, taking you from the beginning to the most advanced topics. Let's get started with Chapter 1 now.

Getting Started: Essential Objective-C

1

This book takes you on a guided tour of Objective-C, from the basics on up through the cool stuff.

Objective-C is a cross-platform language, so you'll find it on many systems: the Mac, of course, but also Linux, UNIX, Windows, and more—and its core programming code stays the same across all those platforms.

Objective-C is actually a layer built on top of the C language, and everything that works in standard (that is, ANSI) C works in Objective-C. Objective-C also adds tons of object-oriented features to the original C language.

The way it uses objects is what makes Objective-C so popular, but just what is an object? Object-oriented programming was introduced when programs began to get very large and the structure of the code began to get in the way. Object-oriented programming lets programmers wrap whole sections of their code into easily handled, self-contained *objects* and so let them break up their code.

continues on next page

For example, say you have a bowl of pudding that you want to keep cold. You could set up a system of coolant pipes, switches, and dials that cool your pudding but which take your constant attention: you have to watch the temperature, and when the pudding gets too warm, you have to turn on the coolant compressor and pump and so on; when the pudding gets cold enough, you have switch those things off.

That was the old way of programming, with the guts of every item in your program laid bare to the whole rest of the program.

Object-oriented programming, by contrast, lets you wrap all that functionality into a single object: a refrigerator. The refrigerator's job is to keep things like pudding cold without a lot of fuss on your part. It is responsible for maintaining its own internal state—that is, remaining cold inside. It has thermostats and relays and the like to automatically handle the jobs you previously did manually. So if you want your pudding kept cold, simply put it in the refrigerator. All the details are hidden from view, and your kitchen becomes a much easier place to handle conceptually.

So it is with object-oriented programming. Now you can wrap code and data together into objects that are self-contained, and because all the details are hidden, your interaction with those objects becomes a lot simpler.

That's the secret behind object-oriented programming: divide and conquer.

In this book, you'll see what makes the objects in Objective-C tick. They're different than the objects in other languages—they communicate with messages; you don't call the code in them directly—but they're just as powerful, and often more so.

We'll start in this chapter with the basics: handling basic data items, printing results from Objective-C programs, running your programs, and more.

Creating Your First Program

We're going to jump right into Objective-C by creating and running a program, which we'll name first.m.

We'll start by creating a function—that is, a bit of code that you can call by name—named `main()`:

```
int main(void)
{
        .
        .
        .
}
```

Functions can be passed data, as you'll see later, but this function isn't passed any data, which is why we use the keyword `void` in the parentheses. Functions can also return values, and the `main()` function returns an integer value to Objective-C indicating whether the program succeeded. The `int` in front of `main()` tells Objective-C to expect an integer return value. The code for the `main()` function goes inside curly braces: { and }.

Next, we'll use the built-in Objective-C function named `printf()` to display some text. We pass the text we want `printf()` to display inside parentheses:

```
int main(void)
{
  printf ("Welcome to Objective-C!");
        .
        .
        .
}
```

continues on next page

✔ **Tip**

- The extension for Objective-C code files is .m.

To use the `printf()` function, we have to tell Objective-C about that function with a function declaration, as you'll see when we discuss how to create functions. The declarations for the standard I/O functions like `printf()` are contained in an Objective-C file named stdio.h, where .h stands for "header file"; we include stdio.h in our program as shown here so Objective-C knows about the `printf()` function:

```
#include <stdio.h>
int main(void)
{
  printf ("Welcome to Objective-C!");
         .
         .
         .
}
```

When the program ends, Objective-C will expect some indication of whether the function succeeded. We'll return a value of 0 to Objective-C, which means there were no errors. **Listing 1.1** shows the entire program, which you will create step by step in the following tasks.

✔ Tip

- Note that `#import` and `#include` are the same for our purposes. You can use them interchangeably and in any order.

```
#include <stdio.h>
int main(void)
{
  printf ("Welcome to Objective-C!");
  return 0;
}
```

Listing 1.1 Your first Objective-C program.

To create your first Objective-C program on the Mac:

1. From http://developer.apple.com/iphone, download and install the Xcode Integrated Development Environment.
2. Run Xcode.
3. Choose File > New Project.
4. In the New Project window, choose Application.
5. Click the Command-Line Tool icon to select it.
6. From the Type drop-down menu, choose Foundation.
7. Click the Choose button.
8. Enter **First** as the name of your application.
9. Select a save location and click the Save button.
10. In the text editor window, enter the code in Listing 1.1.
11. Choose File > Save.

To create your first Objective-C program in Linux, UNIX, or Windows:

1. Open a text editor.
2. Enter the code in Listing 1.1.
3. Save the file as **first.m** in a directory of your choice.

Compiling and Running Your First Program

To run an Objective-C program, you first have to compile it, which makes Objective-C convert your code into the machine language that your computer can understand.

When you run the first program, you should see this result:

```
Welcome to Objective-C!
```

The Objective-C language comes built into Mac OX 10.6, but not Linux, UNIX, or Windows, so you'll have to download it.

If you're using Linux or UNIX, go to http://www.GNUstep.org/resources/sources.html and download and install GNUstep, which gives you the Objective-C compiler.

If you're using Windows, go to http://www.GNUstep.org/experience/Windows.html and download the Windows installer for GNUstep and run it to install GNUstep.

To compile and run your first Objective-C program on the Mac:

1. In Xcode, on the Project window toolbar, click the Build and Run button.

   You should see this message:

   ```
   Welcome to Objective-C!
   ```

Congratulations, you've run your first Objective-C program!

To compile and run your first Objective-C program in Linux or UNIX:

1. Open a command prompt window.
2. Change to the directory containing first.m.
3. Enter the following command, prefacing `gcc` with the path to the GNUstep gcc compiler if your computer can't find the compiler:

   ```
   $ gcc -o first first.m
   ```
4. Run the program, like this:

   ```
   $ ./first
   ```

   You should see this message:

   ```
   Welcome to Objective-C!
   ```

Congratulations, you've run your first Objective-C program!

✔ Tip

- This book uses $ as a generic command prompt.

To compile and run your first Objective-C program in Windows:

1. Choose Start > Programs > GNUstep > Shell.
2. In the shell, change to the directory containing first.m/. For example, if first.m is in the directory C:\objectivec, you would enter the following (where $ is a generic command prompt):

   ```
   $ cd c:\objectivec
   ```
3. In the shell, enter the following command to compile first.m into first.exe:

   ```
   $ gcc -o first first.m
   ```
4. Execute the first.exe program, like this:

   ```
   $ ./first
   ```

   You should see this message:

   ```
   Welcome to Objective-C!
   ```

Congratulations, you've run your first Objective-C program!

Using Variables

In Objective-C programs, you can store your data in variables, which are placeholders for that data.

For example, say you have $1 million in your bank account and want to keep track of it; you can store that amount in a variable named amount, like this:

```
int amount = 1000000;
```

This code creates a variable that stores integers (again, that's the int part) and initializes the value in the amount variable to 1000000.

To display the value in the amount variable, you can use printf():

```
printf ("The amount in your account is
  $%i\n", amount);
```

This code prints the string "The amount in your account is " to start. The %i code is a placeholder that will be replaced by the integer variable that follows the quoted string, which is the amount variable. (The \n entry is the newline code, which makes the text skip to a new line.)

When this program runs, you'll see the value in the amount variable displayed like this:

```
The amount in your account is $1000000
```

To use variables:

1. Enter the code shown in **Listing 1.2** in a new program, **account.m**.
2. Create the new variable named amount and initialize it to 1000000 (**Listing 1.3**).
3. Display the value in the amount variable (**Listing 1.4**).
4. Build and run the account.m program.

   You should see this result:

   ```
   The amount in your account is
   $1000000
   ```

```
#include <stdio.h>
int main(void)
{
        .
        .
        .
}
```

Listing 1.2 Creating account.m.

```
#include <stdio.h>
int main(void)
{
  int amount = 1000000;
        .
        .
        .
}
```

Listing 1.3 Editing account.m.

```
#include <stdio.h>
int main(void)
{
  int amount = 1000000;
   printf ("The amount in your account is
     $%i\n", amount);
   return 0;
}
```

Listing 1.4 Using an integer variable.

Displaying Values in Variables

The capability to display the values stored in variables with the Objective-C built-in `printf()` function is very useful. In the previous task, you saw that the code `%i` is a placeholder for integer variables:

```
printf ("The amount in your account is
  $%i\n", amount);
```

Table 1.1 shows some of the most popular `printf()` codes.

For example, if you change the `amount` variable in the previous task from the integer (`int`) type to a floating-point value (`float`), you can display its value using `printf()` and `%f` (for `float`):

```
#include <stdio.h>
int main(void)
{
  float amount = 1000000;
   printf ("The amount in your account is
     $%f\n", amount);
   return 0;
}
```

In this task, you'll create a program named temperature.m that will display a time (as an integer) and a temperature (as a floating-point number). To do that, you'll use commas in `printf()` to separate the variables whose values you want to display:

```
#include <stdio.h>
int main(void)
{
  int time = 4;
  float temperature = 73.6;
   printf ("At %i o'clock, the temperature
     is %f degrees.\n", time,
     temperature);
   return 0;
}
```

continues on next page

Table 1.1

Common printf() Codes

Code	Display
%i	Integer
%c	Character
%d or %i	Signed decimal integer
%e	Scientific notation (mantissa/exponent) using e character
%E	Scientific notation (mantissa/exponent) using E character
%f	Floating-point decimal
%g	The shorter of %e or %f
%G	The shorter of %E or %f
%s	String of characters
%u	Unsigned decimal integer

Given the finite precision of computers, however, you'll actually see this instead of 73.6 degrees:

```
At 4 o'clock, the temperature is
73.599998 degrees.
```

You need to round the floating-point value up, which you can do by using the code `%4.1f` instead of just `%f`. The code `%4.1f` tells the program that you want your number to be four total places long with one place after the decimal point. That gives you

```
At 4 o'clock, the temperature is 73.6
degrees.
```

which is what you want.

To show variable values:

1. Create a new program named **temperature.m**.
2. In temperature.m, enter the code shown in **Listing 1.5**.
3. Save temperature.m.
4. Run the temperature.m program.
   You should see the following:
   ```
   At 4 o'clock, the temperature is 73.6
   degrees.
   ```

```
#include <stdio.h>
int main(void)
{
  int time = 4;
  float temperature = 73.6;
   printf ("At %i o'clock, the temperature
     is %4.1f degrees.\n", time,
     temperature);
   return 0;
}
```

Listing 1.5 Displaying an `int` and a `float` variable.

Working with Data Types

Objective-C comes with some built-in data types that you can use to create variables. For example, you've already seen the `int` type, which you can use to create integer variables.

The `int` type is called a primitive in Objective-C, because it's built in to the language and it's a simple type. **Table 1.2** shows the primitive types in Objective-C.

In this task, we'll create a program named datatype.m that has four variables: a character, an integer, a long, and a float variable:

```
char c = 'a';
int i = 4;
long l = 123454321;
float f = 3.1415926;
```

The code will display the values of them all:

```
The character is 'a'.
The integer is 4.
The long is 123454321.
The float is  3.141593.
```


Table 1.2

Objective-C Primitive Data Types

TYPE	DESCRIPTION	SIZE
char	A character of the local character set	1 byte (8 bits)
double float	Double precision	8 bytes
float	Floating-point number (for example, 3.1415926)	4 bytes (32 bits)
int	An integer (whole numbers; for example, –1, 100, 34)	4 bytes (32 bits)
long	A double short	4 bytes
long long	A double long	8 bytes
short	A short integer	2 bytes

To display variable values:

1. Create a new program named **datatype.m**.
2. In datatype.m, enter the code shown in **Listing 1.6**.
3. Save datatype.m.
4. Run the datatype.m program.
   You should see the following:
   ```
   The character is 'a'.
   The integer is 4.
   The long is 123454321.
   The float is 3.141593.
   ```

```
#include <stdio.h>

int main(void)
{
  char c = 'a';
  int i = 4;
  long l = 123454321;
  float f = 3.1415926;

   printf("The character is '%c'.\n", c);
   printf ("The integer is %i.\n", i);
   printf ("The long is %i.\n", l);
   printf ("The float is %10.6f.\n", f);

   return 0;
}
```

Listing 1.6 The datatype.m program.

```
#include <stdio.h>

int main(void)
{
  /* Declare
   * the
   * variables.
   */

  char c = 'a';
  int i = 4;
  long l = 123454321;
  float f = 3.1415926;

  /* Display the results. */

  printf ("The character is '%c'.\n", c);
  printf ("The integer is %i.\n", i);
  printf ("The long is %i.\n", l);
  printf ("The float is %10.6f.\n", f);

  return 0;
}
```

Listing 1.7 The datatype.m program with comments.

Adding Comments

Objective-C lets you include English-language comments to yourself or others in programs. Such comments are useful to provide documentation or to indicate how code needs to be modified.

Objective-C ignores any text between the markers /* and */, so you can insert comments like this in your code:

```
/* Here is a comment. */
```

You also can change such comments into multiline comments, like this:

```
/* Here
 * is
 * a
 * comment.
 */
```

Objective-C also recognizes another type of comment that is commonly used in the C++ language: one-line comments that begin with //. Objective-C ignores everything after // on a line, so these comments are often used to annotate single lines of code:

```
int i = 4; //Here is a comment.
```

In this task, we'll add comments to the datatype.m program from the previous task.

To add comments:

1. Open datatype.m for editing.
2. In datatype.m, enter the two comments shown in **Listing 1.7**.

continues on next page

3. In datatype.m, enter the one-line comment shown in **Listing 1.8**.
4. Save datatype.m.
5. Run the datatype.m program to confirm that Objective-C ignores the comments.

```
#include <stdio.h>

int main(void)
{
  /* Declare
   * the
   * variables.
   */

  char c = 'a';
  int i = 4;
  long l = 123454321;  //A long value
  float f = 3.1415926;

  /* Display the results. */

  printf ("The character is '%c'.\n", c);
  printf ("The integer is %i.\n", i);
  printf ("The long is %i.\n", l);
  printf ("The float is %10.6f.\n", f);

  return 0;
}
```

Listing 1.8 The datatype.m program with a single-line comment.

Using Arithmetic Operators

Like most programming languages, Objective-C comes stocked with arithmetic operators to let you perform basic math. These operators let you add values, subtract them, multiply them, and more (**Table 1.3**).

You can use these operators with the values in variables, like this:

```
sum = operand1 + operand2;
```

We'll put together a program, operators.m, to test these operators.

✔ Tip

- If you're not familiar with the modulus operator, %, it just returns the integer remainder after division. For example, since 10 divided by 3 is 3 with a remainder of 1, 10 % 3 = 1.

Table 1.3

Objective-C Arithmetic Operators

Operator	Function
+	Addition
-	Subtraction
/	Division
*	Multiplication
%	Modulus

To use the Objective-C arithmetic operators:

1. Create a new program named **operators.m**.
2. In operators.m, enter the code shown in **Listing 1.9**.

   This code declares two operands: x and y.
3. Add the code to put the arithmetic operators to use (**Listing 1.10**).
4. Save operators.m.
5. Run the operators.m program.

   You should see the following:

```
5 +  2 =  7.
5 -  2 =  3.
5 *  2 = 10.
5 /  2 = 2.5.
```

```
#include <stdio.h>

int main(void)
{

  float x = 5;
  float y = 2;
        .
        .
        .
  return 0;
}
```

Listing 1.9 Starting operators.m.

```
#include <stdio.h>

int main(void)
{

  float x = 5;
  float y = 2;

  printf ("%2.0f + %2.0f = %2.0f.\n",
    x, y, x + y);
  printf ("%2.0f - %2.0f = %2.0f.\n",
    x, y, x - y);
  printf ("%2.0f * %2.0f = %2.0f.\n",
    x, y, x * y);
  printf ("%2.0f / %2.0f = %2.1f.\n",
    x, y, x / y);

  return 0;
}
```

Listing 1.10 The operators.m program using arithmetic operators.

```
#include <stdio.h>

int main(void)
{

  float x = 0;
  float y = 5;
        .
        .
        .
  return 0;
}
```

Listing 1.11 Starting assignment.m.

Using Assignment Operators

You've already seen that you can assign values to variables with the assignment operator =, as shown here:

```
x = 5;
```

You can also combine operators with the assignment operator as a shortcut. For example, you can write

```
x = x + 5;
```

using the shortcut assignment operator + = as shown here:

```
x += 5;
```

Table 1.4 lists the assignment operators.

To use the Objective-C assignment operators:

1. Create a new program named **assignment.m**.
2. In assignment.m, enter the code shown in **Listing 1.11**.

   This code declares two variables: x and y.

continues on next page

Table 1.4

Objective-C Assignment Operators

Operator	Function
=	Assignment
+=	Addition assignment
-=	Subtraction assignment
/=	Division assignment
*=	Multiplication assignment
%=	Modulus assignment

3. Add the code to put the assignment operators to use (**Listing 1.12**).
4. Save assignment.m.
5. Run the assignment program.

   You should see the following:

```
x =  0.
x =  5 --> x:  5.
x +=  5 --> x: 10.
x -=  5 --> x:  5.
x *=  5 --> x: 25.
x /=  5 --> x:  5.
```

```
#include <stdio.h>

int main(void)
{

  float x = 0;
  float y = 5;

  printf ("x = %2.0f.\n", x);

  x = y;
  printf ("x = %2.0f --> x: %2.0f.\n", y,
    x);

  x += y;
  printf ("x += %2.0f --> x: %2.0f.\n",
    y, x);

  x -= y;
  printf ("x -= %2.0f --> x: %2.0f.\n",
    y, x);

  x *= y;
  printf ("x *= %2.0f --> x: %2.0f.\n",
    y, x);

  x /= y;
  printf ("x /= %2.0f --> x: %2.0f.\n",
    y, x);

  return 0;
}
```

Listing 1.12 The assignment.m program using assignment operators.

Using the Increment and Decrement Operators

Objective-C also supports two more operators: the ++ increment operator and the -- decrement operator. For instance, to increment the value in the variable named `temperature`, you write `temperature++`, which adds 1 to the value in `temperature`. To decrement the value, you enter `temperature--`, which decreases the value in `temperature` by 1.

You can use ++ and -- either before or after a variable, and the position makes a difference. The expression `++x` adds 1 to x and then evaluates the rest of the line of code, and the expression `x++` first evaluates the line of code and then, after the current line of code has finished executing, increments the value in x.

For example, say you have this code:

```
float x = 0;
float y = 5;

x = y++;
printf (
  "After x = y++ x: %2.0f y: %2.0f.\n",
 x, y);
```

This code would print `x: 5 y:6`, because the increment operation was performed after the assignment. On the other hand, say you execute:

```
x = ++y;
printf (
  "After x = ++y x: %2.0f y: %2.0f.\n",
  x, y);
```

This code would print `x: 7 y: 7`, because the increment operation was completed first and then the assignment.

Let's test the increment operator.

✔ Tip

- The decrement operator works the same way as the increment operator.

To use the Objective-C increment operator:

1. Create a new program named **increment.m**.
2. In increment.m, enter the code shown in **Listing 1.13**.

   This code declares two variables: x and y.
3. Add the code to put the increment operator to use (**Listing 1.14**).
4. Save increment.m.
5. Run the increment.m program.

   You should see the following:

   ```
   x:  0 y;  5.
   After x = y++ x:  5 y:  6.
   After x = ++y x:  7 y:  7.
   ```

```
#include <stdio.h>

int main(void)
{

  float x = 0;
  float y = 5;
        .
        .
        .
  return 0;
}
```

Listing 1.13 Starting increment.m.

```
#include <stdio.h>

int main(void)
{

  float x = 0;
  float y = 5;

  printf ("x: %2.0f y; %2.0f.\n", x, y);

  x = y++;
  printf (
    "After x = y++ x: %2.0f y: %2.0f.\n",
   x, y);

  x = ++y;
  printf (
    "After x = ++y x: %2.0f y: %2.0f.\n",
    x, y);

  return 0;
}
```

Listing 1.14 The increment.m program using the increment operator.

Changing Type with Cast Operators

Suppose you want to find the modulus of two floating-point numbers in a program named cast.m. You might enter the following code:

```
float x = 5;
float y = 3;
int result = 0;

result = x % y;
```

When you run this code, however, the Objective-C compiler returns an error message:

```
cast.m: In function `main':
cast.m:12: error: invalid operands to
binary %
```

The problem is that the modulus operator needs integer operands. To solve this problem, you can temporarily convert the floating-point variables to integer variables with the `(int)` cast operator, like this:

```
float x = 5;
float y = 3;
int result = 0;

result = (int) x % (int) y;
```

Now everything works fine.

You can use cast operators to convert between various types: `(int)`, `(float)`, `(long)`, and so on.

To use a cast operator:

1. Create a new program named **cast.m**.
2. In cast.m, enter the code shown in **Listing 1.15**.
   This code declares three variables: x, y, and result.
3. Add the code to put the modulus operator and the (int) cast operator to work (**Listing 1.16**).
4. Save cast.m.
5. Run the cast.m program.
   You should see the following:
   ```
   x:  5 y;  3.
   The result of x mod y is 2
   ```

```
#include <stdio.h>

int main(void)
{

  float x = 5;
  float y = 3;
  int result = 0;
        .
        .
        .
  return 0;
}
```

Listing 1.15 Starting cast.m

```
#include <stdio.h>

int main(void)
{

  float x = 5;
  float y = 3;
  int result = 0;

  printf ("x: %2.0f y; %2.0f.\n", x, y);

  result = (int) x % (int) y;
  printf (
    "The result of x mod y is %i\n",
    result);

  return 0;
}
```

Listing 1.16 The cast.m program using a cast operator.

2

Directing Program Flow

This chapter is all about taking control of your code by making programs flow as you want. You'll see how to make choices with the `if` statement, loop over and over with loops, and more.

The primary program flow statement that allows you to make choices is the `if` statement. With the `if` statement, you can test a condition and execute code depending on whether or not the statement is true. For example, say you have a variable named temperature, which is set to 72:

```
#include <stdio.h>
int main(void)
{
  int temperature = 72;
        .
        .
        .
}
```

continues on next page

You can use the == equality operator to test whether the value of the temperature variable is equal to 72 and, if so, execute specific code like this:

```
#include <stdio.h>
int main(void)
{
  int temperature = 72;
  if (temperature == 72)
  {
    printf("Perfect weather.\n");
  }

  return 0;
}
```

You can also add an `else` statement that executes code if the condition in the `if` statement turns out to be false:

```
#include <stdio.h>
int main(void)
{
  int temperature = 78;

  if (temperature == 72)
  {
    printf("Perfect weather.\n");
  }
  else
  {
    printf("Weather could be better.\n");
  }
  return 0;
}
```

Loops provide another tool for controlling the flow of your programs. Loops let you perform specific actions over and over, such as summing a group of numbers or drawing lines. For example, in a `for` loop, the most common type of loop, you initialize a variable called `loop_index` (usually by setting it to zero), specify the condition that causes the loop to end, and an operation to perform after the body of the loop is executed. In the example here, the loop ends when the `loop_index` variable contains a number greater than 5; after the body of the loop runs, the `loop_index` value is incremented:

```
#include <stdio.h>
int main(void)
{
  int loop_index;
  for (loop_index = 0; loop_index < 5;
    loop_index++)
  {
    printf("You'll see this five
      times.\n");
  }

  return 0;
}
```

This example displays the text "You'll see this five times."

More on the `for` loop and the other loops in Objective-C is coming up in this chapter.

Using the if Statement

The `if` statement is the most basic of the program flow control statements. This statement lets you test a condition, and if the condition is true, lets you execute specific code.

For example, if you set a variable named `temperature` to 72, you can use an `if` statement to test to make sure that the variable does contain 72. You place the condition you want to test, which in this case is `temperature == 72`, using the == equality operator, inside parentheses, and the code you want to execute if the condition is true in curly braces following the parentheses, like this:

```
#include <stdio.h>

int main(void)
{
  int temperature = 72;
  if (temperature == 72)
  {
    printf("Perfect weather.\n");
  }
  return 0;
}
```

In this case, the temperature does equal 72, so the code in the curly braces will be executed. Here, that code prints the message "Perfect weather."

To use the Objective-C if statement:

1. Create a new program named **if.m**.
2. In if.m, enter the code shown in **Listing 2.1**.

   This code creates the `temperature` variable and checks to see if it equals 72.
3. Add the code to display the "perfect weather" message if the temperature equals 72 (**Listing 2.2**).
4. Save if.m.
5. Run the if.m program.

   You should see the following:

   `Perfect weather.`

```
#include <stdio.h>

int main(void)
{
  int temperature = 72;

  if (temperature == 72)
  {
      .
      .
      .
  }

  return 0;
}
```

Listing 2.1 Starting if.m.

```
#include <stdio.h>

int main(void)
{
  int temperature = 72;
  if (temperature == 72)
  {
    printf("Perfect weather.\n");
  }

  return 0;
}
```

Listing 2.2 The if.m program.

Using the else Statement

The `if` statement allows you to specify code that runs if a condition you specify (such as `temperature == 72`) is true. The `else` statement lets you specify alternative code that runs when an `if` statement's condition turns out to be false.

For example, as shown here, you can modify the previous task's code to display the message "Weather could be better." if the temperature is not 72.

```
#include <stdio.h>
int main(void)
{
  int temperature = 78;

  if (temperature == 72)
  {
    printf("Perfect weather.\n");
  }
  else
  {
    printf("Weather could be better.\n");
  }
  return 0;
}
```

✔ Tip

- If you use an `else` statement, it must immediately follow an `if` statement.

To use the Objective-C else statement:

1. Create a new program named **else.m**.
2. In else.m, enter the code shown in **Listing 2.3**.

   This code creates the `temperature` variable and checks to see if it equals 72.
3. Add the `else` statement to display alternative text if the temperature does not equal 72 (**Listing 2.4**).
4. Save else.m.
5. Run the else.m program.

   You should see the following:

   `Weather could be better.`

```
#include <stdio.h>
int main(void)
{
  int temperature = 78;

  if (temperature == 72)
  {
    printf("Perfect weather.\n");
  }
        .
        .
        .
  return 0;
}
```

Listing 2.3 Starting else.m.

```
#include <stdio.h>
int main(void)
{
  int temperature = 78;

  if (temperature == 72)
  {
    printf("Perfect weather.\n");
  }
  else
  {
    printf("Weather could be better.\n");
  }
  return 0;
}
```

Listing 2.4 The else.m program.

Using the switch Statement

If you have many conditions to test, you may want to use a `switch` statement instead of multiple `if-else` statements. You can test text strings (coming up in the next chapter) or integers with the `switch` statement. When a `case` statement that matches the value in the variable you're testing is found in the `switch` statement, the corresponding code is executed.

The following example tests for various temperatures, executing code for each temperature:

```
#include <stdio.h>

int main(void)
{
  int temperature = 73;
  switch(temperature)
  {
    case 71:
      printf("Could be a little
        warmer.\n");
      break;
    case 72:
      printf("Perfect weather.\n");
      break;
    case 73:
      printf("It's a little warm.\n");
      break;
    default:
      printf("Unknown temperature.\n");
  }
  return 0;
}
```

To use the Objective-C switch statement:

1. Create a new program named **switch.m**.
2. In switch.m, enter the code shown in **Listing 2.5**.

   This code creates the `temperature` variable and the `switch` statement.
3. Add the `case` statements to display a messages corresponding to the temperature (**Listing 2.6**).
4. Save switch.m.
5. Run the switch.m program.

   You should see the following:

   `It's a little warm.`

✔ Tip

- If no `case` statement matches the variable you're testing, the `default` case is executed.

```
#include <stdio.h>

int main(void)
{
  int temperature = 73;

  switch(temperature)
  {
        .
        .
        .
  }
  return 0;
}
```

Listing 2.5 Starting switch.m.

```
#include <stdio.h>

int main(void)
{
  int temperature = 73;

  switch(temperature)
  {
    case 71:
      printf("Could be a little
        warmer.\n");
      break;
    case 72:
      printf("Perfect weather.\n");
      break;
    case 73:
      printf("It's a little warm.\n");
      break;
    default:
      printf("Unknown temperature.\n");
  }

  return 0;
}
```

Listing 2.6 The switch.m program.

```
#include <stdio.h>

int main(void)
{
  int temperature = 71;

  if (temperature < 72)
  {
        .
        .
        .
  }

  return 0;
}
```

Listing 2.7 Starting compare.m.

```
#include <stdio.h>

int main(void)
{
  int temperature = 71;

  if (temperature < 72)
  {
    printf(
      "Could be a little warmer.\n");
  }

  return 0;
}
```

Listing 2.8 The compare.m program.

Table 2.1

Objective-C Comparison Operators	
OPERATOR	DESCRIPTION
==	Equality
!=	Inequality
>	Greater than
<	Less than
>=	Greater than or equal to
<=	Less than or equal to

Using Comparison Operators

So far we've compared values with the == equality comparison operator:

```
#include <stdio.h>

int main(void)
{
  int temperature = 72;
  if (temperature == 72)
  {
    printf("Perfect weather.\n");
  }

  return 0;
}
```

The equality operator is just one of the Objective-C comparison operators, which are listed in **Table 2.1**.

To use comparison operators:

1. Create a new program named **compare.m**.
2. In compare.m, enter the code shown in **Listing 2.7**.

   This program compares the temperature to 72, and if the temperature is less than 72, it executes code.
3. Add the `case` statements to display a messages if the temperature is below 72 (**Listing 2.8**).
4. Save compare.m.
5. Run the compare.m program.

   You should see the following:

   `Could be a little warmer.`

Using Logical Operators

In the previous task, we checked to see if the temperature was less than 72:

```
#include <stdio.h>

int main(void)
{
  int temperature = 71;

  if (temperature < 72)
  {
    printf(
      "Could be a little warmer.\n");
  }
  return 0;
}
```

What if you want to check whether the temperature is between 70 degrees and 74 degrees? For that, you can use a logical operator. Logical operators let you connect true-or-false clauses. **Table 2.2** lists the logical operators.

To use logical operators:

1. Create a new program named **logical.m**.
2. In logical.m, enter the code shown in **Listing 2.9**.

   This code sets up the `if` statement to check whether the temperature is less than 74 *and* greater than 70.
3. Display a message if the temperature is within the tested range (**Listing 2.10**).
4. Save logical.m.
5. Run the logical.m program.

   You should see the following:

   `Nice weather.`

```
#include <stdio.h>

int main(void)
{
  int temperature = 71;

  if (temperature < 74
    && temperature > 70 )
  {
       .
       .
       .
  }

  return 0;
}
```

Listing 2.9 Starting logical.m.

```
#include <stdio.h>

int main(void)
{
  int temperature = 71;

  if (temperature < 74
    && temperature > 70 )
  {
    printf("Nice weather.\n");
  }

  return 0;
}
```

Listing 2.10 The logical.m program.

Table 2.2

Objective-C Logical Operators

Operator	Description
!	Not. Reverses the true/false value of a condition.
&&	And. Both clauses have to be true for the resulting expression to be true.
||	Or. Either clause can be true for the resulting expression to be true.

Using the Conditional Operator

We've seen how you can make decisions in code using the `if` statement and execute other code to match the results of those decisions.

You can also use the conditional operator to make decisions. This operator lets you evaluate an expression and execute code depending on the result. The conditional operator has this format:

`conditional ? expression1 : expression2;`

Objective-C evaluates *`conditional`*, and if it's true, executes *`espression1`*; if it's false, it executes *`expression2`*. The returned value from this operator is the expression that is executed. For example, you may want to cap the temperature at 72, and if it's greater than 72, set it to 72. Here's how to do that with a conditional operator:

```
#include <stdio.h>

int main(void)
{
  int temperature = 78;
  temperature = temperature > 72 ?
    temperature = 72 : temperature;

  printf("The temperature is %i.\n",
    temperature);

  return 0;
}
```

Here, if the temperature is greater than 72, the first expression, 72, is returned from the conditional operator. If it's less than 72, the temperature itself is returned.

To use the Objective-C conditional operator:

1. Create a new program named **conditional.m**.
2. In conditional.m, enter the code shown in **Listing 2.11**.

   This code creates the `temperature` variable and the statement that uses the conditional operator to make sure the temperature is capped.
3. Add the code to display the results (**Listing 2.12**).
4. Save conditional.m.
5. Run the conditional.m program.

   You should see the following:

   `The temperature is 72.`

```
#include <stdio.h>

int main(void)
{
  int temperature = 78;

  temperature = temperature > 72 ?
    temperature = 72 : temperature;
        .
        .
        .
}
```

Listing 2.11 Starting conditional.m.

```
#include <stdio.h>

int main(void)
{
  int temperature = 78;

  temperature = temperature > 72 ?
    temperature = 72 : temperature;

  printf("The temperature is %i.\n",
    temperature);

  return 0;
}
```

Listing 2.12 The conditional.m program.

Using the for Loop

Loops let computers do what they excel at: perform many operations rapidly. Loops let you execute a section of code over and over, typically operating on different data in each loop *iteration* (that is, each time through the loop).

The for loop has this format:

```
for(initilialization; end_condition;
  after_loop_expression)
{
  body
}
```

Here, *initilization* is an expression evaluated before the loop starts; you typically set a loop_index variable (which keeps track of the number of times the loop has executed) to zero here. The *end_condition* specification is an expression (such as loop_index < 5) that, when it is no longer true, ends the loop. The *after_loop_expression* specification is executed after the body of the loop (in curly braces following the for statement) is executed; you typically increment the loop_index value here.

Here's an example that uses a for loop to display the message "You'll see this five times.":

```
int main(void)
{
  int loop_index;

  for (loop_index = 0; loop_index < 5;
    loop_index++)
  {
    printf(
      "You'll see this five times.\n");
  }

  return 0;
}
```

To use the Objective-C for loop:

1. Create a new program named **for.m**.
2. In for.m, enter the code shown in **Listing 2.13**.

   This code creates a `for` loop that executes five times.
3. Add the code to display the message each time through the loop (**Listing 2.14**).
4. Save for.m.
5. Run the for.m program.

   You should see the following:

```
You'll see this five times.
You'll see this five times.
You'll see this five times.
You'll see this five times.
You'll see this five times.
```

```
int main(void)
{
  int loop_index;

  for (loop_index = 0; loop_index < 5;
    loop_index++)
  {
      .
      .
      .
  }

  return 0;
}
```

Listing 2.13 Starting for.m.

```
int main(void)
{
  int loop_index;

  for (loop_index = 0; loop_index < 5;
    loop_index++)
  {
    printf(
      "You'll see this five times.\n");
  }

  return 0;
}
```

Listing 2.14 The for.m program.

Using the while Loop

Objective-C offers another popular loop: the `while` loop. This loop keeps executing its body while a certain condition is true. The `while` loop has this format:

```
while(condition)
{
  body
}
```

The `while` loop checks the *`condition`* expression, and it it's true, executes the code in the body of the loop. When the condition is tested and turns out to be false, the loop stops executing.

Here's an example of a `while` loop that displays the message "You'll see this five times.":

```
#include <stdio.h>

int main(void)
{
  int loop_index = 0;

  while (loop_index < 5)
  {
    printf("You'll see this five
      times.\n");
    loop_index++;
  }

  return 0;
}
```

To use the Objective-C while loop:

1. Create a new program named **while.m**.
2. In while.m, enter the code shown in **Listing 2.15**.

   This code creates a `while` loop that executes five times.
3. Add the code to display the message each time through the loop and to increment `loop_index`, which is checked by the `while` loop before each loop iteration (**Listing 2.16**).
4. Save while.m.
5. Run the while.m program.

   You should see the following:

   ```
   You'll see this five times.
   You'll see this five times.
   You'll see this five times.
   You'll see this five times.
   You'll see this five times.
   ```

```
#include <stdio.h>

int main(void)
{
  int loop_index = 0;

  while (loop_index < 5)
  {
        .
        .
        .
  }

  return 0;
}
```

Listing 2.15 Starting while.m.

```
#include <stdio.h>

int main(void)
{
  int loop_index = 0;

  while (loop_index < 5)
  {
    printf("You'll see this five
      times.\n");
    loop_index++;
  }

  return 0;
}
```

Listing 2.16 The while.m program.

Using the do...while Loop

One more popular loop that Objective-C offers is the `do...while` loop. Like the `while` loop, this loop keeps executing its body while a certain condition is true, but unlike the `while` loop, it checks its condition *after* the loop's body executes. The `do...while` loop has this format:

```
do {
  body
} while(condition);
```

The `do...while` loop executes its body and then checks the *`condition`* expression; it it's true, the loop executes again. When the condition is tested and turns out to be false, the loop stops executing.

Why do you need the `do...while` loop in addition to the `while` loop? You typically use a `do...while` loop when the loop condition is set for the first time within the loop: for example, if you're reading from a file and terminating the loop at the end of the file, you need to try to read from the file at least once to see if the file contains any data for you to read before the loop is terminated.

Here's an example that displays the message "You'll see this five times." This time, a `do...while` loop was used:

```
#include <stdio.h>

int main(void)
{
  int loop_index = 0;

  do {
    printf(
      "You'll see this five times.\n");
    loop_index++;
  } while (loop_index < 5);

  return 0;
}
```

To use the Objective-C do...while loop:

1. Create a new program named **do.m**.
2. In do.m, enter the code shown in **Listing 2.17**.

   This code creates a `do...while` loop that executes five times.
3. Add the code to display the message each time through the loop and to increment `loop_index`, which is checked by the `do...while` loop after each loop iteration (**Listing 2.18**).
4. Save do.m.
5. Run the do.m program.

   You should see the following:

```
You'll see this five times.
You'll see this five times.
You'll see this five times.
You'll see this five times.
You'll see this five times.
```

```
#include <stdio.h>

int main(void)
{
  int loop_index = 0;

  do {
        .
        .
        .
  } while (loop_index < 5);

  return 0;
}
```

Listing 2.17 Starting do.m,

```
#include <stdio.h>

int main(void)
{
  int loop_index = 0;

  do {
    printf(
      "You'll see this five times.\n");
    loop_index++;
  } while (loop_index < 5);

  return 0;
}
```

Listing 2.18 The do.m program.

Using the break Statement

Sometimes you may want to break out of a loop—that is, terminate it. For example, say that you're happily printing the reciprocals of –1/5 up to 1/5:

```
#include <stdio.h>

int main(void)
{
  float loop_index;

  for (loop_index = 5; loop_index > -5;
    loop_index--)
  {
    printf("1/%2.1f = %10.6f\n",
      loop_index, 1.0/loop_index);
  }

  return 0;
}
```

However, when you get to 1/0 (division by zero), Objective-C will report an error. To avoid that, you can use a `break` statement to break the loop execution before the attempt to divide by 0 occurs:

```
#include <stdio.h>
int main(void)
{
  float loop_index;

  for (loop_index = 5; loop_index > -5;
    loop_index--)
  {
    if (loop_index == 0.0) {
      break;
    }
    printf("1/%2.1f = %10.6f\n",
      loop_index, 1.0/loop_index);
  }

  return 0;
}
```

The `break` statement causes the loop to end—in this case, avoiding division by zero,

To use the Objective-C break statement:

1. Create a new program named **break.m**.
2. In break.m, enter the code shown in **Listing 2.19**.

   This code prints the reciprocals from –1/5 to 1/5, but will report an error for 1/0.
3. Add the code to break loop execution before the attempt to divide by zero (**Listing 2.20**).
4. Save break.m.
5. Run the break.m program.

   You should see the following:

   ```
   1/5.0 =   0.200000
   1/4.0 =   0.250000
   1/3.0 =   0.333333
   1/2.0 =   0.500000
   1/1.0 =   1.000000
   ```

```
#include <stdio.h>

int main(void)
{
  float loop_index;
  for (loop_index = 5; loop_index > -5;
    loop_index--)
  {
    printf("1/%2.1f = %10.6f\n",
      loop_index, 1.0/loop_index);
  }

  return 0;
}
```

Listing 2.19 Starting break.m.

```
#include <stdio.h>
int main(void)
{
  float loop_index;

  for (loop_index = 5; loop_index > -5;
    loop_index--)
  {
    if (loop_index == 0.0) {
      break;
    }
    printf("1/%2.1f = %10.6f\n",
      loop_index, 1.0/loop_index);
  }

  return 0;
}
```

Listing 2.20 The break.m program.

3 Handling Data

This chapter is all about working with data in Objective-C. You'll use arrays, pointers, strings, and more.

An array is a set of data items, called elements, that you can refer to with an array index. For example, if you store numbers in an array named `array`, you can address each element with an index number like this: `array[0]`, which refers to the first element; `array[1]`, which refers to the second element; and so on. The following code creates an array of five elements, stores a value of 51 in `array[0]`, and then displays that value:

```
#include <stdio.h>
int main(){
  int array[5];
  array[0] = 51;
  printf("array[0] is %i.\n", array[0]);
  return 0;}
```

Pointers are special variables that hold the address in memory of data items. You can store the address of a variable named `integer` in a pointer with the & operator like this:

```
  pointer = &integer;
```

continues on next page

You can then refer to the value of integer as *pointer like this:

```
#include <stdio.h>
int main(){
  int integer, *pointer;
  integer = 1;
  pointer = &integer;
  *pointer = 2;
  printf(
    "The value of the integer is: %i",
    *pointer);
  return 0;}
```

Pointers are very important in Objective-C because you use them to create objects. For example, text strings in Objective-C are usually NSString objects (the "NS" part stands for NeXtStep, the name of the organization that originally created these objects). To create a text string in Objective-C, you create a pointer to a NSString object. You can pass that object the message cString to have it return a C-style string that printf() can print:

```
#include <stdio.h>
#include <Foundation/Foundation.h>
int main(void){
  NSString *helloString =
    @"Hello there.";
  printf("%s\n", [helloString cString]);
  return 0;}
```

✔ Tip

- Here's an important point: To create objects of any class that begins with NS, you must include the Objective-C Foundation header file (the #include <Foundation/Foundation.h> line in the code here).

About Creating NS-Class Objects

To create objects of any class that begins with `NS`, you must include the Objective-C Foundation header file. If you're using Xcode on the Mac, make sure that the Foundation option is selected on the New Project page when you create a project. If you're using Objective-C in Windows, Linux, or UNIX, you need a makefile named GNUmakefile like the following, which compiles a program named source.m and creates an executable application named app (which is app.exe in Windows):

```
include $(GNUSTEP_MAKEFILES)/common.make
TOOL_NAME = app
app_OBJC_FILES = source.m
include $(GNUSTEP_MAKEFILES)/tool.make
```

In Linux and UNIX (not Windows), you also have to set up the GNUstep environment variables. You do that in the C shell like this:

```
source <GNUstep root>/System/Library/
Makefiles/GNUstep.csh
```

And you do it like this in the Bourne shell:

```
. <GNUstep root>/System/Library/
Makefiles/GNUstep.sh
```

On most UNIX systems, <GNUstep root> is /usr/lib/GNUstep. To run the makefile, just change to the directory with the makefile (GNUmakefile) and type **make**, which creates the executable application in a subdirectory named obj. In this example, you can run that application by typing **./obj/app**.

Creating Arrays

Arrays are sets of elements (which can be of any Objective-C type) that you can access using an index value. In the following task, you'll declare an array of five elements, assign the value 51 to the first element, `array[0]`, and then display that value.

To create an Objective-C array:

1. Create a new program named **array.m**.
2. In array.m, enter the code shown in **Listing 3.1**.

   This code creates the array named `array` and sets `array[0]` equal to 51.
3. Add the code to display the value in `array[0]` (**Listing 3.2**).
4. Save array.m.
5. Run the array.m program.

   You should see the following:

   `array[0] is 51`

```
#include <stdio.h>

int main()
{
  int array[5];

  array[0] = 51;
        .
        .
        .
  return 0;
}
```

Listing 3.1 Starting array.m.

```
#include <stdio.h>

int main()
{
  int array[5];

  array[0] = 51;

  printf("array[0] is %i.\n",
    array[0]);

  return 0;
}
```

Listing 3.2 The array.m program.

Initializing Arrays

You can initialize the value of the elements in an array when you declare that array by enclosing the initialization values in curly braces:

```
#include <stdio.h>

int main()
{
  int scores[5] = {92 , 73 , 57 , 98 ,
    89 };

  printf(
    "The array is %i elements long.",
    sizeof(scores) / sizeof(int));

  return 0;
}
```

To initialize an array:

1. Create a new program named **initializearray.m**.
2. In initializearray.m, enter the code shown in **Listing 3.3**.

   This code creates the array and initializes the values of its elements.
3. Calculate the number of elements in the array, using the `sizeof` operator to get the size of the whole array and dividing by the size of a single element (**Listing 3.4**).
4. Save initializearray.m.
5. Run the initializearray.m program.

   You should see the following:

   `The array is 5 elements long.`

```
#include <stdio.h>

int main()
{
  int scores[5] = {92 , 73 , 57 , 98 ,
    89 };
        .
        .
        .
  return 0;
}
```

Listing 3.3 Starting initializearray.m.

```
#include <stdio.h>

int main()
{
  int scores[5] = {92 , 73 , 57 , 98 ,
    89 };

  printf(
    "The array is %i elements long.",
    sizeof(scores) / sizeof(int));

  return 0;
}
```

Listing 3.4 The initializearray.m program.

Looping over Arrays

Arrays and loops are made for each other. Arrays hold sets of data, and loops let you iterate over such data sets. Looping over long sets of data in arrays is one of the things computers are really good at.

For example, if you have an array of student scores and want to find their average, you can use a `for` loop:.

```
int student_index, scores[5] =
  { 92 , 73 , 57 , 98 , 89 };
float sum = 0;

for (student_index = 0, sum = 0;
  student_index < 5; student_index++)
{
  sum += scores[student_index];
}

printf("Average score is %2.1f",
  sum / 5);
```

To loop over an array:

1. Create a new program named **arrayloop.m**.
2. In arrayloop.m, enter the code shown in **Listing 3.5**.

   This code creates the `scores` array and initializes it.
3. Add the code to sum all the elements in the array and find their average (**Listing 3.6**).
4. Save arrayloop.m.
5. Run the arrayloop.m program.

   You should see the following:

   ```
   Average score is 81.8
   ```

```
#include <stdio.h>

int main()
{
  int student_index, scores[5] =
    { 92 , 73 , 57 , 98 , 89 };
  float sum = 0;
        .
        .
        .
  return 0;
}
```

Listing 3.5 Starting arrayloop.m.

```
#include <stdio.h>

int main()
{
  int student_index, scores[5] =
    { 92 , 73 , 57 , 98 , 89 };
  float sum = 0;

  for (student_index = 0, sum = 0;
    student_index < 5; student_index++)
  {
    sum += scores[student_index];
  }

  printf("Average score is %2.1f",
    sum / 5);

  return 0;
}
```

Listing 3.6 The arrayloop.m program.

Creating Two-Dimensional Arrays

So far we've been working with arrays in one dimension, but you can create multi-dimensional arrays as well. While you access an element in a one-dimensional array as `array[element_number]`, you access elements in a two-dimensional array as `array[row][column]`.

For example, if you have an array of student scores for each of three tests and want to find the average score for each of the three tests, you can use a two-dimensional array. You initialize the two-dimensional array with nested lists in curly braces and loop over the lists with nested `for` loops:

```
int test_index, student_index,
  scores[3][5] = {
  { 92 , 73 , 57 , 98 , 89 },
  { 88 , 76 , 23 , 95 , 72 },
  { 94 , 82 , 63 , 99 , 94 }
};
float sum;
for (test_index = 0; test_index < 3;
  test_index++)
{
  for (student_index = 0, sum = 0;
    student_index
    < 5; student_index++)
  {
    sum +=
     scores[test_index][student_index];
  }
  printf(
    "Average for test %i is %2.1f.\n",
    test_index + 1, sum / 5);
}
```

To create a two-dimensional array:

1. Create a new program named **array2.m.**
2. In array2.m, enter the code shown in **Listing 3.7**.

   This code creates an array and loops over each row.
3. Add the code to loop over each column and display the average for each test (**Listing 3.8**).
4. Save array2.m
5. Run the array2.m program.

   You should see the following:

   ```
   Average for test 1 is 81.8
   Average for test 2 is 70.8
   Average for test 3 is 86.4
   ```

```
#include <stdio.h>

int main()
{
  int test_index, student_index,
    scores[3][5] = {
    { 92 , 73 , 57 , 98 , 89 },
    { 88 , 76 , 23 , 95 , 72 },
    { 94 , 82 , 63 , 99 , 94 }
  };
  float sum;
  for (test_index = 0; test_index < 3;
    test_index++)
  {
        .
        .
        .
  }
  return 0;
}
```

Listing 3.7 Starting array2.m.

```
#include <stdio.h>
int main()
{
  int test_index, student_index,
    scores[3][5] = {
    { 92 , 73 , 57 , 98 , 89 },
    { 88 , 76 , 23 , 95 , 72 },
    { 94 , 82 , 63 , 99 , 94 }
  };
  float sum;

  for (test_index = 0; test_index < 3;
    test_index++)
  {
    for (student_index = 0, sum = 0;
      student_index
      < 5; student_index++)
    {
      sum +=
       scores[test_index][student_index];
    }
    printf(
      "Average for test %i is %2.1f.\n",
      test_index + 1, sum / 5);
  }
  return 0;
}
```

Listing 3.8 The array2.m program.

```
#include <stdio.h>

int main()
{
  int integer, *pointer;

  integer = 1;

  pointer = &integer;
        .
        .
        .
  return 0;
}
```

Listing 3.9 Starting pointers.m.

```
#include <stdio.h>

int main()
{
  int integer, *pointer;

  integer = 1;

  pointer = &integer;

  *pointer = 2;

  printf(
    "The value of the integer is: %i",
    *pointer);

  return 0;
}
```

Listing 3.10 The pointers.m program.

Using Pointers

Pointers hold the address in memory of data items. You declare a pointer by prefacing it with an asterisk (*):

```
int integer, *pointer;
```

Then you can use the & operator to get the address of a variable in memory and assign it to the pointer:

```
integer = 1;

pointer = &integer;
```

Using the asterisk again, you can refer to the data pointed to by the pointer::

```
*pointer = 2;
```

To use pointers:

1. Create a new program named **pointers.m**.
2. In pointers.m, enter the code shown in **Listing 3.9**.

   This code creates the pointer and assigns it the address of the variable named `integer`.
3. Assign a new value to the memory location pointed to by the pointer and display the data stored in that location (**Listing 3.10**).
4. Save pointers.m.
5. Run the pointers.m program.

   You should see the following:

   `The value of the integer is: 2`

Using Pointer Math

If you point to items arranged one after another in memory, such as in an array, you can increment or decrement pointers to point to the next or previous item. For instance, the following example prints the first number in an array and then the second number by incrementing a pointer:

```
float values[4] = {0.0, 1.0, 2.0,
  3.0};

float *pointer = &values[0];

printf("*pointer = %2.1f\n", *pointer);

printf("*(++pointer) = %2.1f",
  *(++pointer));
```

To use pointer math:

1. Create a new program named **pointermath.m**.
2. In pointermath.m, enter the code shown in **Listing 3.11**.

   This code simply points to the first item in the array and prints it.
3. Add the code to increment the pointer and display the next element in the array (**Listing 3.12**).
4. Save pointermath.m.
5. Run the pointermath.m program.

   You should see the following:

   ```
   *pointer = 0.0
   *(++pointer) = 1.0
   ```

```
#include <stdio.h>

int main()
{
  float values[4] = {0.0, 1.0, 2.0,
    3.0};

  float *pointer = &values[0];

  printf("*pointer = %2.1f", *pointer);
        .
        .
        .
}
```

Listing 3.11 Starting pointermath.m.

```
#include <stdio.h>

int main()
{
  float values[4] = {0.0, 1.0, 2.0,
    3.0};

  float *pointer = &values[0];

  printf("*pointer = %2.1f\n", *pointer);

  printf("*(++pointer) = %2.1f",
    *(++pointer));

  return 0;
}
```

Listing 3.12 The pointermath.m program.

```
#include <stdio.h>

int main()
{
  double values[10];

  double *pointer = values;

  pointer[2] = 3.14159;
        .
        .
        .
}
```

Listing 3.13 Starting pointersarray.m.

```
#include <stdio.h>

int main()
{
  double values[10];

  double *pointer = values;

  pointer[2] = 3.14159;

  printf("values[2] = %10.6f",
    values[2]);

  return 0;
}
```

Listing 3.14 The pointersarray.m program.

Interchanging Pointers and Arrays

Array names and pointers are in many ways interchangeable in Objective-C. For example, you can create an array, assign the name of the array to a pointer, and treat the pointer as you would the array name:

```
double values[10];

double *pointer = values;

pointer[2] = 3.14159;
```

To use arrays as pointers:

1. Create a new program named **pointersarray.m**.
2. In pointersarray.m, enter the code shown in **Listing 3.13**.

   This code creates an array and assigns the array name to a pointer.
3. Add the code to display the value of the assigned element (**Listing 3.14**).
4. Save pointersarray.m.
5. Run the pointersarray.m program.

   You should see the following:

   ```
   values[2] =   3.141590
   ```

Using Strings

You might think that Objective-C comes with a built-in string data type, much like the built-in types `float` and `char`, but it doesn't. Instead, Objective-C uses the Foundation class `NSString`.

You first include the Foundation classes (which means you have to use a makefile in Windows, Linux, and UNIX); then you can create a string object of class `NSString`. As with all Objective-C objects, you get a pointer to the object and can initialize your string like this:

```
#include <Foundation/Foundation.h>

  NSString *helloString =
    @"Hello there.";
```

The @ sign in front of the quoted text indicates that you want to use an Objective-C style of string, not the default C-style of strings (Objective-C strings have a lot more power built into them than C strings do).

To use Objective-C strings:

1. Create a new program named **string.m**.
2. In string.m, enter the code shown in **Listing 3.15** to create and display a string.

   To print the string with `printf()`, you're converting the string to a C-style string by sending it the message `cString` (you communicate with Objective-C objects by sending them messages in this way).

```
#include <stdio.h>
#include <Foundation/Foundation.h>

int main(void)
{
  NSString *helloString =
    @"Hello there.";

  printf("%s\n", [helloString cString]);

  return 0;
}
```

Listing 3.15 Creating string.m.

```
include $(GNUSTEP_MAKEFILES)/common.make

TOOL_NAME = string
string_OBJC_FILES = string.m

include $(GNUSTEP_MAKEFILES)/tool.make
```

Listing 3.16 The GNUmakefile file.

3. Save string.m.
4. If you're using Linux, UNIX, or Windows, create a makefile named **GNUmakefile**, as shown in **Listing 3.16**, and follow the directions in "About Creating NS-Class Objects" earlier in this chapter to compile string.m with the makefile.
5. Save GNUmakefile.
6. Compile and run the string.m program (in Linux, UNIX, and Windows, you run the program as ./obj/string).

   You should see the following:

   ```
   Hello there.
   ```

Passing Messages to String Objects

As with other Objective-C objects, you communicate with NSString objects by passing them messages. For example, passing a string the message length returns its length, and passing it the message getSubstringFromIndex lets you get a substring.

For example, if you want to convert a string that contains an integer into an actual integer, you use the intValue message, which you send like this:

```
printf("The number is %i\n",
[numberString intValue]);
```

To call Objective-C string methods:

1. Create a new program named **stringtoint.m**.
2. In stringtoint.m, enter the code shown in **Listing 3.17**.

   This code creates a string named numberString, initializes it, and then sends it the message intValue to convert it to an integer and print that integer.
3. Save stringtoint.m.
4. If you're using Linux, UNIX, or Windows, create a makefile named **GNUmakefile**, as shown in **Listing 3.18**, and follow the directions in "About Creating NS-Class Objects" earlier in this chapter to compile stringtoint.m with the makefile.
5. Save GNUmakefile.
6. Compile and run the stringtoint.m program (in Linux, UNIX, and Windows, you run the program as ./obj/string).

   You should see the following:

   ```
   The number is 5
   ```

```
#include <stdio.h>
#include <Foundation/Foundation.h>

int main(void)
{
  NSString *numberString = @"5";

  printf("The number is %i\n", [numberString
  intValue]);

  return 0;
}
```

Listing 3.17 Creating stringtoint.m.

```
include $(GNUSTEP_MAKEFILES)/common.make

TOOL_NAME = stringtoint
stringtoint_OBJC_FILES = stringtoint.m

include $(GNUSTEP_MAKEFILES)/tool.make
```

Listing 3.18 The GNUmakefile file.

✔ Tips

- You can find all the messages NSString objects can take at http://developer.apple.com/mac/library/documentation/Cocoa/Reference/Foundation/Classes/NSString_Class/Reference/NSString.html.
- A function like intValue that's built into an object is called a *method*.

```
#include <stdio.h>

int main()
{
  enum day
  {
    Sunday,
    Monday,
    Tuesday,
    Wednesday,
    Thursday,
    Friday,
    Saturday
  };

  enum day today = Friday;
        .
        .
        .
}
```

Listing 3.19 Starting enumeration.m.

Using Enumerations

Objective-C lets you define your own named types, called enumerations. For example, you can tell Objective-C that an enumeration named day holds values named for the days of the week, like this:

```
enum day
{
  Sunday,
  Monday,
  Tuesday,
  Wednesday,
  Thursday,
  Friday,
  Saturday
};
```

You can then assign a variable of that type to one of those values:

```
enum day today = Friday;
```

To create an enumeration:

1. Create a new program named **enumeration.m**.
2. In enumeration.m, enter the code shown in **Listing 3.19**.

   This code creates the enumeration and assigns the variable today to one of the allowed named values.

continues on next page

3. Add the code to test whether today is Friday (**Listing 3.20**).
4. Save enumeration.m.
5. Run the enumeration.m program.

   You should see the following:

   `Today is Friday.`

```
#include <stdio.h>

int main()
{
  enum day
  {
    Sunday,
    Monday,
    Tuesday,
    Wednesday,
    Thursday,
    Friday,
    Saturday
  };

  enum day today = Friday;

  if(today == Friday){
    printf("Today is Friday.");
  }

  return 0;
}
```

Listing 3.20 The enumeration.m program.

Creating Functions

This chapter is all about functions, which are chunks of code you can call to make them run—and they won't run unless you call them.

So far, the code in the programs we've discussed has executed automatically when the programs start. But functions are different; you have to explicitly call a function by name in your code before its code will run. That means that using functions, you can divide your code into smaller parts: the divide and conquer technique.

In Objective-C, functions are a crucial stop on the way to building your own objects. Objects let you package both data and functions—called methods when they're built into objects—together, as you'll soon see.

Here is an example of how you might create a function named `greeter()`:

```
#include <stdio.h>

void greeter(void)
{
  printf("Hello there.");
}
        .
        .
        .
```

Note the function's structure: In front of its name (here, `greeter`), you specify a return type, which indicates the type of the data item

continues on next page

that the function can return. Since `greeter()` doesn't return any data, the return type is `void`.

Then, in parentheses following the name comes a list of arguments; these are the data items you pass to the function to let it do its work. Since the `greeter()` function takes no arguments, it uses `void` for the argument list as well. Then comes the body of the function—the actual code that runs when you call the function—enclosed in curly braces: { and }. In this case, the `greeter()` function simply displays a message: "Hello there."

The whole thing—the line that gives the function's return type, name, and argument list, as well as the body of the function—is called the function's *definition.*

You can call the `greeter()` function by name to run it from the code in `main()`—which itself is a function:

```
#include <stdio.h>

void greeter()
{
  printf("Hello there.");
}

int main()
{
  greeter();

  return 0;
}
```

Now when your program runs, it will start automatically by calling the `main()` function. The code in the `main()` function includes a call to the `greeter()` function, which then will display its message. Nice.

You'll get the full story on functions here: how to pass data to them, how to return data from them, how to pass pointers to them to access the data in the calling code directly, how to make them call themselves (a process called recursion), and how to set up pointers to them and then call them using those pointers.

```
#include <stdio.h>

void greeter()
{
  printf("Hello there.");
}
        .
        .
        .
```

Listing 4.1 Starting function.m.

```
#include <stdio.h>

void greeter()
{
  printf("Hello there.");
}

int main()
{
  greeter();

  return 0;
}
```

Listing 4.2 The function.m program.

Defining a Function

In this first task, we'll put to work the example introduced in the chapter opener: the `greeter()` function.

To create a function:

1. Create a new program named **function.m**.
2. In function.m, enter the code shown in **Listing 4.1**.

   This code creates the `greeter()` function.
3. Add the code shown in **Listing 4.2**.

   This code adds the `main()` function and the call to the `greeter()` function.
4. Save function.m.
5. Run the function.m program.

   You should see the following:

   `Hello there.`

Declaring Functions Using Prototypes

In the previous example, we defined the function in the code before calling it, so Objective-C knew about the `greeter()` function before it was called. But the function definition can also come after the call to that function in your code, like this:

```
#include <stdio.h>

int main()
{
  greeter();

  return 0;
}

void greeter()
{
  printf("Hello there.");
}
```

In this case, you must tell Objective-C about the `greeter()` function with a function *prototype*:

```
#include <stdio.h>

void greeter(void);

int main()
{
  greeter();

  return 0;
}

void greeter()
{
  printf("Hello there.");
}
```

```
#include <stdio.h>

void greeter(void);
        .
        .
        .
void greeter()
{
  printf("Hello there.");
}
```

Listing 4.3 Starting functionprototype.m.

```
#include <stdio.h>

void greeter(void);

int main()
{
  greeter();

  return 0;
}

void greeter()
{
  printf("Hello there.");
}
```

Listing 4.4 The functionprototype.m program.

A function prototype is just like the line where you declare a function (the line just before the function body inside curly braces), except that you remove the names of any function arguments (leaving just their types) and end the prototype with a semicolon.

The function prototype is also called the function *declaration* (as opposed to the function definition, which includes the body of the function).

You can also put function prototypes in header files, whose names end with .h, and then include them with stdio.h as shown in the listings here. That `include` statement includes the stdio.h header file, which includes prototypes for functions such as `printf()`.

To create a function prototype:

1. Create a new program named **functionprototype.m**.
2. In functionprototype.m, enter the code shown in **Listing 4.3**.

   This code creates the `greeter()` function after the `main()` function and adds a prototype before the `main()` function so Objective-C knows about the `greeter()` function.
3. Add the `main()` function to call the `greeter()` function (**Listing 4.4**).
4. Save functionprototype.m.
5. Run the functionprototype.m program.

   You should see the following:

   `Hello there.`

Passing Arguments to Functions

You can pass data to functions so they can work on that data. For example, you can create a function named `adder()` that you want to add two integers and display the results.

To indicate which arguments a function takes, you include an argument list in the parentheses following the function name when you define the function. For example, the `adder()`function takes two arguments: the two integers to add, which we'll name x and y:

```
void adder(int x, int y)
```

Now in the body of the function, you can refer to the first argument as x and the second argument as y.

When you create a function prototype, on the other hand (when you call the function before defining it in your code), you omit the names of the arguments, instead including just the type:

```
void adder(int, int);
```

Now you can write the body of the `adder()` function to add the two integers, which you can refer to by name, x and y:

```
void adder(int x, int y)
{
  printf("%i + %i = %i", x, y, x + y);
}
```

✔ Tip

- You specify the type (`int` here) of every argument in the list just before its name.

```
#include <stdio.h>

void adder(int x, int y)
{
  printf("%i + %i = %i", x, y, x + y);
}
        .
        .
        .
```

Listing 4.5 Starting functionargs.m.

```
#include <stdio.h>

void adder(int x, int y)
{
  printf("%i + %i = %i", x, y, x + y);
}

int main()
{
  int value1 = 5, value2 = 10;

  adder(value1, value2);

  return 0;
}
```

Listing 4.6 The functionargs.m program.

To pass arguments to a function:

1. Create a new program named **functionargs.m**.
2. In functionargs.m, enter the code shown in **Listing 4.5**.

   This code creates the `adder()` function.
3. Enter the code to specify the `main()` function and the call to the `adder()` function to add 5 plus 10 (**Listing 4.6**).
4. Save functionargs.m.
5. Run the functionargs.m program.

   You should see the following:

   `5 + 10 = 15`

Returning Values from Functions

In addition to passing data to functions, you can have functions return data. They can return a single data item—an integer, for example—or an array or an object.

To indicate that a function returns a value, you specify the type of that data value first in a function definition or declaration. For example, you can alter the `adder()` function from the previous task to return an integer value holding the sum of the two values passed to it, like this:

```
int adder(int x, int y)
```

To actually return the sum of the two values passed to the `adder()` function, you use a `return` statement:

```
int adder(int x, int y)
{
  return x + y;
}
```

That's how it works: to return a value from a function, you place the value you want to return right after the keyword `return`.

Now when you call the `adder()` function and pass data to that function, the call itself will be replaced by the function's return value. So to add 5 and 10 and display the results, you can use this code:

```
  int value1 = 5, value2 = 10;

  printf("%i + %i = %i", value1, value2,
    adder(value1, value2));
```

```
#include <stdio.h>

int adder(int x, int y)
{
  return x + y;
}
       .
       .
       .
```

Listing 4.7 Starting functionreturn.m.

```
#include <stdio.h>

int adder(int x, int y)
{
  return x + y;
}

int main()
{
  int value1 = 5, value2 = 10;

  printf("%i + %i = %i", value1, value2,
    adder(value1, value2));

  return 0;
}
```

Listing 4.8 The functionreturn.m program.

To return values from functions:

1. Create a new program named **functionreturn.m**.
2. In functionreturn.m, enter the code shown in **Listing 4.7**.

   This code creates the `adder()` function and sets it up to return the sum of the two integers passed to it.
3. Add the code to call the `adder()` function and pass two integers to it (**Listing 4.8**).
4. Save functionreturn.m.
5. Run the functionreturn.m program.

   You should see the following:

   `5 + 10 = 15`

Using Function Scope

Scope refers to the range of visibility of data items. Functions define their own scope. That is, when you define a variable in a function, it becomes a local variable for that function and takes precedence over other versions of the same variable. For example, you can define an integer named `number` and set it to 1 like this:

```
int number = 1;
```

And then you can also define an integer named `number` inside a function:

```
int number = 1;

void function(void)
{
  int number = 2;
  printf(
    "In the function the number is %i\n",
    number);
}
```

The local version of `number` will take precedence in the function, so here the `printf()` statement will display a value of 2 for `number`. If `number` hadn't been defined locally in the function, the version from outside the function would have been used, and the `printf()` statement would have shown a value of 1.

In Objective-C, any code block—that is, code enclosed in curly braces such as function bodies or the bodies of `if` statements—defines its own scope, so local variables will always take precedence over variables defined outside the code block.

To use function scope:

1. Create a new program named **functionscope.m**.
2. In functionscope.m, enter the code shown in **Listing 4.9**.

   This code declares an integer named `number` displays its value in `main()`, and then calls a function.

```
#include <stdio.h>
void function(void);
int number = 1;
int main()
{
  printf("In main the number is %i\n",
    number);
  function();
  return 0;
}
        .
        .
        .
```

Listing 4.9 Starting functionscope.m.

```
#include <stdio.h>
void function(void);
int number = 1;
int main()
{
  printf("In main the number is %i\n",
    number);
  function();
  return 0;
}

void function(void)
{
  int number = 2;

  printf(
    "In the function the number is %i\n",
    number);

    {
      int number = 3;;
      printf(
      "In the block the number is %i\n",
      number);
    }
    printf(
    "After the block the number is %i\n",
    number);
}
```

Listing 4.10 The functionscope.m program.

3. Add the function that redefines `number` locally as well as in a code block (**Listing 4.10**).
4. Save functionscope.m.
5. Run the functionscope.m program. You should see the following:

```
In main the number is 1
In the function the number is 2
In the block the number is 3
After the block the number is 2
```

Passing Pointers to Functions

When you pass a pointer to a function, that function can use the pointer to change data in the calling code. For instance, here's an example that passes a pointer to a function that changes a variable:

```
  int data = 1;

  int* datapointer = &data;

  printf("Before changer(), data = %i\n",
    data);

  changer(datapointer);

  printf("After changer(), data = %i\n",
    data);

void changer(int* pointer)
{
  *pointer = 2;
}
```

To pass a pointer to a function:

1. Create a new program named **functionpasspointers.m**.
2. In functionpasspointers.m, enter the code shown in **Listing 4.11**.

   This code passes a pointer to a function named changer().

```
#include <stdio.h>
void changer(int*);

int main()
{
  int data = 1;

  int* datapointer = &data;

  printf("Before changer(), data = %i\n",
    data);

  changer(datapointer);

  printf("After changer(), data = %i\n",
    data);

  return 0;
}
        .
        .
        .
```

Listing 4.11 Starting functionpasspointers.m.

```
#include <stdio.h>
void changer(int*);

int main()
{
  int data = 1;

  int* datapointer = &data;

  printf("Before changer(), data = %i\n",
    data);

  changer(datapointer);

  printf("After changer(), data = %i\n",
    data);

  return 0;
}

void changer(int* pointer)
{
  *pointer = 2;
}
```

Listing 4.12 The functionpasspointers.m program.

3. Add the code for the `changer()` function, which changes the data back in the calling code (**Listing 4.12**).
4. Save functionpasspointers.m.
5. Run the functionpasspointers.m program. You should see the following:

```
Before changer(), data = 1
After changer(), data = 2
```

Passing Arrays to Functions

You can also pass arrays to functions. For instance, the following example adds the elements of an array and returns the sum:

```
  int data[] = {1, 2, 3, 4};

  int total = adder(data,
    sizeof(data)/sizeof(int));

  printf("The total is %i\n", total);

long adder(int array[], int number_
elements)
{
  long sum = 0;
  int loop_index;

  for (loop_index = 0; loop_index <
    number_elements; loop_index++)
      sum = sum + array[loop_index];

  return sum;
}
```

To pass arrays to functions:

1. Create a new program named **functionpassarrays.m**.
2. In functionpassarrays.m, enter the code shown in **Listing 4.13**.

   This code creates an array and passes it to a function named `adder()`.

```
#include <stdio.h>

long adder(int array[], int number_elements);

int main()
{
  int data[] = {1, 2, 3, 4};

  int total = adder(data,
    sizeof(data)/sizeof(int));

  printf("The total is %i\n", total);

  return 0;
}
```

Listing 4.13 Starting functionpassarrays.m.

```
#include <stdio.h>

long adder(int array[], int number_elements);

int main()
{
  int data[] = {1, 2, 3, 4};

  int total = adder(data,
    sizeof(data)/sizeof(int));

  printf("The total is %i\n", total);

  return 0;
}

long adder(int array[], int number_elements)
{
  long sum = 0;
  int loop_index;

  for (loop_index = 0; loop_index <
    number_elements; loop_index++)
      sum = sum + array[loop_index];

  return sum;
}
```

Listing 4.14 The functionpassarrays.m program.

3. Add the code to create the `adder()` function (**Listing 4.14**).
4. Save functionpassarrays.m.
5. Run the functionpassarrays.m program. You should see the following:
   `The total is 10`

Passing Constant Data to Functions

As you know, if you pass pointers to functions, those functions can change the data to which the pointers point. Since arrays can double as pointers, if you pass an array as a pointer in a function, the function can change your original array. To avoid that, when you pass a copy of your array to the function, mark it as a constant so it can't be changed. You mark data as constant with the `const` keyword:

```
  int data[] = {1, 2, 3, 4};

  int total = adder(data,
    sizeof(data)/sizeof(int));

  printf("The total is %i\n", total);

long adder(const int array[], int
number_elements)
{
  long sum = 0;
  int loop_index;

  for (loop_index = 0; loop_index <
    number_elements; loop_index++)
      sum = sum + array[loop_index];

  return sum;
}
```

In this task, we'll modify the previous task's code to use constant arrays.

To pass constant arrays to functions:

1. Create a new program named **functionpassconstarrays.m**.
2. In functionpassconstarrays.m, enter the code shown in **Listing 4.15**.

   This code creates an array and passes it to a function named `adder()` whose prototype indicates that it takes constant arrays.

```
#include <stdio.h>

long adder(const int array[], int number_
elements);

int main()
{
  int data[] = {1, 2, 3, 4};

  int total = adder(data,
    sizeof(data)/sizeof(int));

  printf("The total is %i\n", total);

  return 0;
}
```

Listing 4.15 Starting functionpassconstarrays.m.

```
#include <stdio.h>

long adder(const int array[], int number_
elements);

int main()
{
  int data[] = {1, 2, 3, 4};

  int total = adder(data,
    sizeof(data)/sizeof(int));

  printf("The total is %i\n", total);

  return 0;
}

long adder(const int array[], int number_
elements)
{
  long sum = 0;
  int loop_index;

  for (loop_index = 0; loop_index <
    number_elements; loop_index++)
      sum = sum + array[loop_index];

  return sum;
}
```

Listing 4.16 The functionpassconstarrays.m program.

3. Add the code to create the `adder()` function, marking the array passed to this function as a constant in the function's argument list (**Listing 4.16**).
4. Save functionpassconstarrays.m.
5. Run the functionpassconstarrays.m program.

   You should see the following:

   `The total is 10`

Using Recursion

Functions can call themselves in Objective-C, a process called recursion, and this process is often useful. For example, say you're writing a function that calculates factorials: for example, 6! =6 x 5 x 4 x 3 x 2 x 1 = 720. Here's a function that calls itself recursively to figure out factorials:

```
int factorial(int value)
{
  if (value == 1) {
    return value;
  } else {
    return value * factorial(value - 1);
  }
}
```

Let's use this function to calculate 6!.

To use recursion:

1. Create a new program named **functionrecursion.m**.
2. In functionrecursion.m, enter the code shown in **Listing 4.17**.

   This code calls the `factorial()` function, passing it a value of 6.
3. Add the code to implement the recursive `factorial()` function (**Listing 4.18**).
4. Save functionrecursion.m.
5. Run the functionrecursion.m program.

   You should see the following:

   `6! = 720`

```
#include <stdio.h>

int main()
{
    printf("6! = %i\n", factorial(6));

    return 0;
}
```

Listing 4.17 Starting functionrecursion.m.

```
#include <stdio.h>

int factorial(int value);

int main()
{
    printf("6! = %i\n", factorial(6));

    return 0;
}

int factorial(int value)
{
  if (value == 1) {
    return value;
  } else {
    return value * factorial(value - 1);
  }
}
```

Listing 4.18 The functionrecursion.m program.

```
#include <stdio.h>

void printem(void);

void caller_function(void (*pointer_to_
function)(void));

int main()
{
    caller_function(printem);

    return 0;
}

void printem(void)
{
    printf("Hello there");;
}
```

Listing 4.19 Starting functionpointers.m.

Using Pointers to Functions

In Objective-C, function names are actually pointers. You can pass function names to other functions, and in the receiving function, you can call the passed function name if you treat it as a pointer.

For example, you can pass function names to this function, named `caller_function()`, and it will call the passed function:

```
void caller_function(void (*pointer_to_
function)(void))
{
    (*pointer_to_function)();
}
```

To call a function pointer:

1. Create a new program named **functionpointers.m**.
2. In functionpointers.m, enter the code shown in **Listing 4.19**.

   This code sets up a function named `printem()` and passes its name to `caller_function()`.

continues on next page

3. Add the code to implement `caller_function()`, which will call the function pointer you pass to it (**Listing 4.20**).
4. Save functionpointers.m.
5. Run the functionpointers.m program. You should see the following:

```
Hello there
```

```
#include <stdio.h>

void printem(void);

void caller_function(void (*pointer_to_
function)(void));

int main()
{
    caller_function(printem);

    return 0;
}

void printem(void)
{
    printf("Hello there");
}

void caller_function(void (*pointer_to_
function)(void))
{
    (*pointer_to_function)();
}
```

Listing 4.20 The functionpointers.m program.

5

Classes and Objects

As discussed in Chapter 1, object-oriented programming was introduced to let you handle bigger programming problems, letting you package programming components into easily remembered objects.

The example used in Chapter 1 was a refrigerator. Instead of starting the pumps, regulating the temperature, and starting the compressor yourself in open code, you wrap all those actions into an object containing data (such as the temperature) and methods (that is, functions, such as `startCompressor()`) into an easily remembered object: a refrigerator. You just put food in the refrigerator, and the refrigerator cools it for you; all the implementation details are hidden from view.

Objective-C object-oriented programming (OOP) lets you use classes and objects. Classes are like cookie cutters—they specify the cookies you can create—and those cookies are the objects. So you first create a class that specifies the data and methods (that is, built-in functions) for your objects, and then you create objects of that class.

continues on next page

Objective-C has its own syntax for classes and objects, and if you haven't programmed in Objective-C before, this syntax will take a little time to learn. Here's an example that we'll dissect in this chapter. This example defines a class, then creates an object of that class, then stores an integer in that object, and then prints the stored integer:

```
#include <stdio.h>
#include <Foundation/Foundation.h>
@interface Container: NSObject
{
  int number;
}
-(void) setNumber: (int) n;
-(int) intValue;
@end
@implementation Container
-(void) setNumber: (int) n
{
    number = n;
}
-(int) intValue
{
  return number;
}
@end
int main(void)
{
  Container *object = [Container new];
  [object setNumber: 5];
  printf("The number is %i\n", [object
  intValue]);
  return 0;
}
```

The result of this code looks like this:

```
The number is 5
```

Besides using this different syntax, you communicate with objects by sending them messages, not by calling object methods directly. For example, to send a message to the `setNumber` method of an object named `object` to set its internally stored number to 5, you send a message like this: `[object setNumber: 5]`.

Objective-C classes are usually based on the Foundation class `NSObject`, so if you're using Linux, UNIX, or Windows, you need to create a GNUmakefile, make sure you're in the same directory as that file, and type **`make`** in the GNUstep shell (see the introduction to Chapter 3 for more information about setting up the environment variables to use `make`). If you enter code in a file named *xxxx*.m, your GNUmakefile file should look like this:

```
include $(GNUSTEP_MAKEFILES)/common.make
TOOL_NAME = xxxx
xxxx_OBJC_FILES = xxxx.m
include $(GNUSTEP_MAKEFILES)/tool.make
```

Then to run your code, enter this at the GNUstep command prompt:

```
./obj/xxxx
```

Creating Objective-C Classes and Objects

In this task, you'll see how to create classes and objects to get an overview of the Objective-C syntax. The subsequent tasks will fill in the details.

To create a class and object:

1. Create a new program file with the extension **.m**.
2. To create a class, you create an `@interface` section, which lists the data in the class and the method prototypes, and an `@implementation` section, which supplies the bodies of the methods, using the syntax shown in **Listing 5.1**.

```
#include <Foundation/Foundation.h>
@interface class_name: NSObject
{
  data_type variable_name;
  data_type variable_name;
}
-(return_type) object_method_name;
+(return_type) class_method_name;
@end

@implementation class_name
-(return_type) object_method_name
{
  [code]
}
+(return_type) class_method_name
{
  [code]
}
@end
```

Listing 5.1 Creating the class.

```
#include <Foundation/Foundation.h>
@interface class_name: NSObject
{
  data_type variable_name;
  data_ptype variable_name;
}
-(return_type) object_method_name;
+(return_type) class_method_name;
@end

@implementation class_name
-(return_type) object_method_name
{
  [code]
}
+(return_type) class_method_name
{
  [code]
}
@end

int main(void)
{
  [class_name class_method_name];
  class_name *object = [class_name new];
  [object object_method_name];
  return 0;
}
```

Listing 5.2 Using a class method and creating an object.

3. In the `main()` function, you execute the class methods by sending *`class_name`* the name of the method as a message: `[`*`class_name class_method_name`*`]`. You can also create objects, handled as pointers in Objective-C, with the new message, like this: *`class_name *object`* `=` `[`*`class_name`* `new]`. Then you can execute object methods by sending the object the method name as a message, like this: `[object object_method_name]`. **Listing 5.2** shows the code.

✔ Tip

- Class methods (defined with a "+" in front of their names) can be run using just the class name, while object methods (defined with a "-" in front of their names) require you to create an object before you run them.

Using Class Methods

A class method is a method you can execute using just the class name—no object is required. You define class methods with a plus sign, "+", in front of their names in both the class's `@interface` section and `@implementation` section, as shown here, where a class returns some text:

```
#include <stdio.h>
#include <Foundation/Foundation.h>

@interface Container
+ (const char *) classMethod;
@end

@implementation Container
+ (const char *) classMethod
{
  return "Hello there.";
}
@end
```

Now you can execute the class method by sending the class the name of the method as a message, like this:

```
int main(void)
{
  printf("%s\n", [Container
    classMethod]);
  return 0;
}
```

You'll see this example at work in this task.

```
#include <stdio.h>
#include <Foundation/Foundation.h>

@interface Container
+ (const char *) classMethod;
@end

@implementation Container
+ (const char *) classMethod
{
  return "Hello there.";
}
@end
        .
        .
        .
```

Listing 5.3 Starting classmethod.m.

```
#include <stdio.h>
#include <Foundation/Foundation.h>

@interface Container
+ (const char *) classMethod;
@end

@implementation Container
+ (const char *) classMethod
{
  return "Hello there.";
}
@end

int main(void)
{
  printf("%s\n", [Container
    classMethod]);
  return 0;
}
```

Listing 5.4 The classmethod.m program.

To create and execute a class method:

1. Create a new program named **classmethod.m**.
2. In classmethod.m, enter the code shown in **Listing 5.3**.

   This code creates a class named `Container` with one method, `classMethod`, which returns a string.
3. Add the `main()` function to execute `classMethod` and display the returned string (**Listing 5.4**).
4. Save classmethod.m.
5. Run the classmethod.m program.

   You should see the following:

   `Hello there.`

Creating an Object

In this task, you'll start creating objects. Here, you'll simply create a class with an empty `@interface` section (while indicating that the class is derived from the `NSObject` class) and an empty `@implementation` section:

```
@interface FirstClass : NSObject

@end

@implementation FirstClass

@end
```

You'll create an object by passing the class the `new` message and then display the message "Object created." as shown here:

```
FirstClass *object = [FirstClass new];
printf("Object created.\n");
return 0;
```

To create an object:

1. Create a new program named **object.m**.
2. In **object.m**, enter the code shown in **Listing 5.5**.

   This code creates the `FirstClass` class.
3. Add the code to create the new object of the `FirstClass` class and display a message indicating that the object has been created (**Listing 5.6**).
4. Save object.m.
5. Run the object.m program (disregard the warning about not using the variable "object" when you compile the code).

   You should see the following:

   `Object created.`

```
#include <stdio.h>
#include <Foundation/Foundation.h>

@interface FirstClass : NSObject

@end

@implementation FirstClass

@end
        .
        .
        .
```

Listing 5.5 Starting object.m.

```
#include <stdio.h>
#include <Foundation/Foundation.h>

@interface FirstClass : NSObject

@end

@implementation FirstClass

@end

int main(void)
{
  FirstClass *object = [FirstClass new];
  printf("Object created.\n");
  return 0;
}
```

Listing 5.6 The object.m program.

```
#include <stdio.h>
#include <Foundation/Foundation.h>

@interface ClassWithMethod : NSObject
- (const char *) stringValue;
@end

@implementation ClassWithMethod
- (const char *) stringValue;
{
  return "Hello there.";
}
@end
        .
        .
        .
```

Listing 5.7 Starting objectmethod.m.

```
#include <stdio.h>
#include <Foundation/Foundation.h>

@interface ClassWithMethod : NSObject
- (const char *) stringValue;
@end

@implementation ClassWithMethod
- (const char *) stringValue;
{
  return "Hello there.";
}
@end

int main(void)
{
  ClassWithMethod *object =
    [ClassWithMethod new];
  printf("%s\n", [object stringValue]);
  return 0;
}
```

Listing 5.8 The objectmethod.m program.

Creating Object Methods

While you can execute a class method with just the name of the class, you need an object to be able to execute object methods—and object methods are more useful because class methods have restrictions on how they store data that object methods don't. You define an object method in a class by preceding its prototype and definition with a minus sign, "-", in both the `@interface` section and `@implementation` section, as shown here, where we create an object method named `stringValue` that returns a string:

```
@interface ClassWithMethod : NSObject
- (const char *) stringValue;
@end

@implementation ClassWithMethod
- (const char *) stringValue;
{
  return "Hello there.";
}
@end
```

To create an object method:

1. Create a new program named **objectmethod.m**.
2. In objectmethod.m, enter the code shown in **Listing 5.7**.

   This code creates the `ClassWithMethod` class and the `stringValue` method in that class.
3. Add the code to execute the `stringValue` object method from the `main()` function (**Listing 5.8**).
4. Save objectmethod.m.
5. Run the objectmethod.m program.

   You should see the following:

   `Hello there.`

Storing Data in Objects

In the previous task, you saw how to set up a method in an object. But objects can contain both methods and data. In this task, you'll see how to store data in objects. You'll also see how to pass arguments to object methods.

You set up your data in variables in the `@interface` section. Then your code can access those variables by name in the methods in the `@implementation` section. For example, the code here stores an integer:

```
@interface Container: NSObject
{
  int number;
}
-(void) setNumber: (int) n;
-(int) intValue;
@end

@implementation Container
-(void) setNumber: (int) n
{
    number = n;
}
@end
```

Then you can execute an object of this class, sending it the value 5 to store:

```
[object setNumber: 5];
```

To store data in an object:

1. Create a new program named **objectdata.m**.
2. In objectdata.m, enter the code shown in **Listing 5.9**.

   This code sets up an internal integer named `number` and a method named `setNumber` to store a value in that integer.

```
#include <stdio.h>
#include <Foundation/Foundation.h>

@interface Container: NSObject
{
  int number;
}
-(void) setNumber: (int) n;
-(int) intValue;
@end

@implementation Container
-(void) setNumber: (int) n
{
    number = n;
}

-(int) intValue
{
  return number;
}
@end
        .
        .
        .
```

Listing 5.9 Starting objectdata.m.

```
#include <stdio.h>
#include <Foundation/Foundation.h>

@interface Container: NSObject
{
  int number;
}
-(void) setNumber: (int) n;
-(int) intValue;
@end

@implementation Container
-(void) setNumber: (int) n
{
    number = n;
}

-(int) intValue
{
  return number;
}
@end

int main(void)
{
  Container *object = [Container new];
  [object setNumber: 5];
  printf("The number is %i\n", [object
    intValue]);
  return 0;
}
```

Listing 5.10 The objectdata.m program.

3. Create an object, set the value of the internally stored number, and display that number (**Listing 5.10**).
4. Save objectdata.m.
5. Run the objectdata.m program.
   You should see the following:
   `The number is 5`

Passing Multiple Arguments to Methods

When you pass multiple arguments to a method, you can name the arguments to keep them straight. For example, you can create a method that takes two numbers and name the second argument `second` (you can choose any name):

```
-(void) setNumbers: (int) n1 second:
    (int) n2;
```

Then when you call this method, you specify the value for the second argument by name:

```
[object setNumbers: 5 second: 10];
```

To pass a multiple arguments to a method:

1. Create a new program named **multipleargs.m**.
2. In multipleargs.m, enter the code shown in **Listing 5.11**.

   This code creates the `setNumbers` method, which can take two arguments.

```
#include <stdio.h>
#include <Foundation/Foundation.h>
@interface Container: NSObject
{
  int number1;
  int number2;
}
-(void) setNumbers: (int) n1 second:
    (int) n2;
-(int) intValue1;
-(int) intValue2;
@end
@implementation Container
-(void) setNumbers: (int) n1 second:
    (int) n2
{
    number1 = n1;
    number2 = n2;
}
-(int) intValue1
{
  return number1;
}
-(int) intValue2
{
  return number2;
}
@end
```

Listing 5.11 Starting multipleargs.m.

```
#include <stdio.h>
#include <Foundation/Foundation.h>
@interface Container: NSObject
{
  int number1;
  int number2;
}
-(void) setNumbers: (int) n1 second:
    (int) n2;
-(int) intValue1;
-(int) intValue2;
@end

@implementation Container
-(void) setNumbers: (int) n1 second:
    (int) n2
{
    number1 = n1;
    number2 = n2;
}
-(int) intValue1
{
  return number1;
}
-(int) intValue2
{
  return number2;
}
@end

int main(void)
{
  Container *object = [Container new];
  [object setNumbers: 5 second: 10];
  printf("The first number is %i\n",
    [object intValue1]);
  printf("The second number is %i\n",
    [object intValue2]);
  return 0;
}
```

Listing 5.12 The multipleargs.m program.

3. Add the code to call the `setNumbers` method (**Listing 5.12**).
4. Save multipleargs.m.
5. Run the multipleargs.m program.
   You should see the following:
   ```
   The first number is 5
   The second number is 10
   ```

Storing the Interface in a Header File

In Objective-C, it's common to put the interface part of a class declaration (the part declared by the `@interface` keyword) in its own header file with the extension .h. To keep things simple, we've not been doing that here, but the process is easy. You just store the `@implementation` section of a class in a file such as header.h:

```
#include <Foundation/Foundation.h>
@interface Container: NSObject
{
  int number;
}
-(void) setNumber: (int) n;
-(int) intValue;
@end
```

Then you include header.h in your program:

```
#include "header.h"
```

To store the interface in a header file:

1. Create a new program named **header.m**.
2. In header.m, enter the code shown in **Listing 5.13**.

   This code is just our example that lets you store numbers in an object, with the interface section in header.h (make sure you use the line `#include "header.h"` at the top of the code).

```
#include "header.h"
#include <stdio.h>
#include <Foundation/Foundation.h>

@implementation Container
-(void) setNumber: (int) n
{
    number = n;
}

-(int) intValue
{
  return number;
}
@end

int main(void)
{
  Container *object = [Container new];
  [object setNumber: 5];
  printf("The number is %i\n", [object
    intValue]);
  return 0;
}
```

Listing 5.13 The header.m program.

```
#include <Foundation/Foundation.h>
@interface Container: NSObject
{
  int number;
}
-(void) setNumber: (int) n;
-(int) intValue;
@end
```

Listing 5.14 The header.h file.

3. Save header.m.
4. Create header.h in the same directory as header.m and add the code shown in **Listing 5.14**.
5. Save header.h.
6. Run the header.m program.

   You should see the following:

   ```
   The number is 5
   ```

Adding the Implementation to the Header File

Objective-C lets you store a class's implementation (the part that follows the `@implementation` keyword) in a header file in addition to its interface (see the previous task).

To store the interface and implementation in a header file:

1. Create a new program named **header2.m**.
2. In header2.m, enter the code shown in **Listing 5.15**.

   This code creates an object of the `Container` class, which is declared and defined in header2.h.
3. Save header2.m.
4. Add the code for the interface and implementation of the `Container` class to header2.h (**Listing 5.16**).
5. Save header2.h.
6. Run the header2.m program.

   You should see the following:

   `The number is 5`

```
#include "header2.h"
#include <stdio.h>
#include <Foundation/Foundation.h>

int main(void)
{
  Container *object = [Container new];
  [object setNumber: 5];
  printf("The number is %i\n", [object
intValue]);
  return 0;
}
```

Listing 5.15 The header2.m program.

```
#include <Foundation/Foundation.h>
@interface Container: NSObject
{
  int number;
}
-(void) setNumber: (int) n;
-(int) intValue;
@end

@implementation Container
-(void) setNumber: (int) n
{
    number = n;
}
-(int) intValue
{
  return number;
}
@end
```

Listing 5.16 The header2.h file.

```
#include "container.h"
#include <stdio.h>
#include <Foundation/Foundation.h>

int main(void)
{
  Container *object = [Container new];
  [object setNumber: 5];
  printf("The number is %i\n",
  [object intValue]);
  return 0;
}
```

Listing 5.17 The main.m program.

```
#include <Foundation/Foundation.h>
@interface Container: NSObject
{
  int number;
}
-(void) setNumber: (int) n;
-(int) intValue;
@end
```

Listing 5.18 The container.h file.

Linking Multiple Files

You can link together multiple files to create a single executable file. You simply need to modify your make file (GNUmakefile) to list all the .m files, like this:

```
include $(GNUSTEP_MAKEFILES)/common.make

TOOL_NAME = main
main_OBJC_FILES = main.m container.m

include $(GNUSTEP_MAKEFILES)/tool.make
```

In this task, you'll create an executable file based on three files: main.m, container.h, and container.m.

To link multiple files:

1. Create a new program named **main.m**.
2. In main.m, enter the code shown in **Listing 5.17**.
3. Save main.m.
4. Create a new file named **container.h**.
5. In container.h, enter the code shown in **Listing 5.18**.
6. Save container.h.
7. Create a new file named **container.m**.

continues on next page

8. In container.m, enter the code shown in **Listing 5.19**.

9. Save container.m.

10. Create a new file named **GNUmakefile**.

11. In GNUmakefile, enter the code shown in **Listing 5.20**.

12. Save GNUmakefile.

13. Run the main.m program.

    You should see the following:

    `The number is 5`

```
#include "container.h"
#include <Foundation/Foundation.h>

@implementation Container
-(void) setNumber: (int) n
{
    number = n;
}
-(int) intValue
{
  return number;
}
@end
```

Listing 5.19 The container.m program.

```
include $(GNUSTEP_MAKEFILES)/common.make

TOOL_NAME = main
main_OBJC_FILES = main.m container.m

include $(GNUSTEP_MAKEFILES)/tool.make
```

Listing 5.20 The GNUmakefile file.

```
#include <stdio.h>
#include <Foundation/Foundation.h>

@interface Container: NSObject
{
  int number;
}
-(void) setNumber: (int) n;
-(int) intValue;
-(Container*) init: (int) n;
@end
        .
        .
        .
```

Listing 5.21 Starting constructor.m.

Using Constructors

In Objective-C, as in many OOP languages, you can use *constructors*, which are special methods used to initialize the data in an object when you create that object. Constructors can be named anything, but they're often named `init`. The constructor returns a pointer to the object, and you get that pointer by calling the super class's `init` method (the super class is the class from which the current class is derived, typically `NSObject`):

```
-(Container*) init: (int) n
{
    self = [super init];

    if ( self ) {
        [self setNumber: n];
    }

    return self;
}
```

In your code, you can then pass values to the constructor when you create an object. For example, the following code initializes the number stored in the object to 3:

```
Container *object = [[Container new]
  init: 3];
```

To use a constructor:

1. Create a new program named **constructor.m**.
2. In constructor.m, enter the code shown in **Listing 5.21**.

   This code starts constructor.m with the interface of the `Container` class.

continues on next page

3. Enter the code to add the implementation of the class methods and use the constructor method to create a new `Container` object and initialize the integer stored internally in that object to 3 (**Listing 5.22**).

4. Save constructor.m.

5. Run the constructor.m program.

   You should see the following:

   `The number is 3`

```
#include <stdio.h>
#include <Foundation/Foundation.h>

@interface Container: NSObject
{
  int number;
}
-(void) setNumber: (int) n;
-(int) intValue;
-(Container*) init: (int) n;
@end

@implementation Container
-(void) setNumber: (int) n
{
    number = n;
}

-(int) intValue
{
  return number;
}

-(Container*) init: (int) n
{
    self = [super init];

    if ( self ) {
        [self setNumber: n];
    }

    return self;
}
@end

int main(void)
{
  Container *object = [[Container new]
    init: 3];
  printf("The number is %i\n", [object
    intValue]);
  return 0;
}
```

Listing 5.22 The constructor.m program.

6 Object-Oriented Programming

In this chapter, we take a deeper look at object-oriented programming in Objective-C.

We start by using *access specifiers*—`@public` (the default), `@private`, and `@protected`—to set the access allowed to members (both methods and data members such as variables) of an object.

We also explore how to use *class variables*—that is, variables that are associated with a class, not just an object (in fact, all objects of that class share the class variables).

Polymorphism refers to using the same code for different kinds of objects, and we see how that works in Objective-C, too.

In addition, we explore how to check whether an object supports a particular method before trying to use that method, how to determine the class of an object—and more.

About Access Specifiers

There are three access specifiers: `@public` (the default), which puts no restriction on the scope of a member; `@private`, which restricts access to code that is in the class in which the member is declared; and `@protected`, which restricts access to code that is in the class in which the member is defined and classes derived from that class

So, for example, you can use this code to access an object's public variable outside that object:

```
#import <stdio.h>
#import <Foundation/NSObject.h>

@interface Access: NSObject {
@public
    int publicVariable;
}
@end

@implementation Access
@end

int main(void)
{
  Access *a = [Access new];

  a->publicVariable = 1;
  printf( "The public variable is %i\n",
  a->publicVariable );

  return 0;
}
```

✔ Tip

- See Chapter 7, "Working with Object-Oriented Inheritance" for a discussion of how to derive one class from another.

Here, we're accessing the public variable as `a->publicVariable`. You use the arrow notation to access members of an object, given a pointer (`a` here) to the object. You'll also need a GNUmakefile file if you're running in Linux, UNIX, or Windows:

```
include $(GNUSTEP_MAKEFILES)/common.make

TOOL_NAME = access
access_OBJC_FILES = access.m

include $(GNUSTEP_MAKEFILES)/tool.make
```

However, declaring a variable private restricts access to just code in its class implementation, which means that this code won't compile:

```
#import <stdio.h>
#import <Foundation/NSObject.h>

@interface Access: NSObject {
@private
    int privateVariable;
}
@end

@implementation Access
@end

int main(void)
{
  Access *a = [Access new];

  a->privateVariable = 2;
  printf( "The private variable is
  %i\n", a->privateVariable );

  return 0;
}
```

You'll see how to use all three access specifiers in the upcoming tasks.

Using Public Access

Public access is the default for object members, but you can also indicate that any members are public with the `@public` access specifier.

To use public access:

1. Create a new program file named **access.m**.
2. Enter the code to create a new class called `Access` with one public member (**Listing 6.1**).
3. Access the public member in the `main()` function (**Listing 6.2**).
4. Save access.m.
5. Run the access.m program.
   You should see the following:
   `The public variable is 1`

```
#import <stdio.h>
#import <Foundation/NSObject.h>

@interface Access: NSObject {
@public
    int publicVariable;
}
@end

@implementation Access
@end

        .
        .
        .
```

Listing 6.1 Creating access.m.

```
#import <stdio.h>
#import <Foundation/NSObject.h>

@interface Access: NSObject {
@public
    int publicVariable;
}
@end

@implementation Access
@end

int main(void)
{
  Access *a = [Access new];

  a->publicVariable = 1;
  printf( "The public variable is %i\n",
    a->publicVariable );

  return 0;
}
```

Listing 6.2 The access.m program.

```
#import <stdio.h>
#import <Foundation/NSObject.h>

@interface Access: NSObject {
@public
    int publicVariable;
@private
    int privateVariable;
@end

@implementation Access
@end
        .
        .
        .
```

Listing 6.3 Starting access.m.

Using Private Access

You make class members private with the `@private` access specifier. Making members private restricts access to them to the code in the class in which they are declared.

To use private access:

1. Open the access.m program from the previous task for editing.
2. In access.m, enter the new code highlighted in **Listing 6.3**.

   This code creates a private data member.

continues on next page

3. Add code to try to access the private data member from outside the object (**Listing 6.4**).
4. Save access.m.
5. Try to run access.m.

   When you try to compile access.m, you'll get either a warning or a hard error (depending on your version of Objective-C and the platform it's running on), because you're trying to access a private member from outside an object. (Note that the warnings will become hard errors in the future.)

```
#import <stdio.h>
#import <Foundation/NSObject.h>

@interface Access: NSObject {
@public
    int publicVariable;
@private
    int privateVariable;
@end

@implementation Access
@end

int main(void)
{
  Access *a = [Access new];

  a->publicVariable = 1;
  printf( "The public variable is %i\n",
    a->publicVariable );

  a->privateVariable = 2;
  printf( "The private variable is
    %i\n", a->privateVariable );

  return 0;
}
```

Listing 6.4 The access.m program.

```
#import <stdio.h>
#import <Foundation/NSObject.h>

@interface Access: NSObject {
@public
    int publicVariable;
@private
    int privateVariable;
@protected
    int protectedVariable;
}
@end

@implementation Access
@end
        .
        .
        .
}
```

Listing 6.5 Starting access.m.

Using Protected Access

You make class members protected with the `@protected` access specifier. Making members protected restricts access to them to the code in the class in which they are declared and classes based on that class.

To use protected access:

1. Open the access.m program from the previous task for editing.
2. In access.m, enter the new code highlighted in **Listing 6.5**.

   This code creates a protected data member.

continues on next page

3. Add the code shown in **Listing 6.6**, which attempts to access the protected member from outside its containing object.
4. Save access.m.
5. Try to run access.m,

   When you try to compile access.m, you'll get either a warning or a hard error (depending on your version of Objective-C and the platform it's running on), because you're trying to access a protected member from outside an object. (Note that the warnings will become hard errors in the future.)

```
#import <stdio.h>
#import <Foundation/NSObject.h>

@interface Access: NSObject {
@public
    int publicVariable;
@private
    int privateVariable;
@protected
    int protectedVariable;
}
@end

@implementation Access
@end

int main(void)
{
  Access *a = [Access new];

  a->publicVariable = 1;
  printf( "The public variable is %i\n",
    a->publicVariable );

  //a->privateVariable = 2;
  //printf( "The private variable is
    %i\n", a->privateVariable );

  a->protectedVariable = 3;
  printf(
    "The protected variable is  %i\n",
    a->protectedVariable );

  return 0;
}
```

Listing 6.6 The object.m program.

```
#import <stdio.h>
#import <Foundation/NSObject.h>

@interface TheClass: NSObject
static int count;
+(int) getCount;
@end

@implementation TheClass
-(TheClass*) init
{
    self = [super init];
    count++;
    return self;
}

+(int) getCount
{
    return count;
}
@end
        .
        .
        .
```

Listing 6.7 Starting classvariables.m.

Using Class Variables

You can create class variables for use with your classes, but there's a hitch: every object of that class shares the same variable, so if one object changes a class variable, that variable is changed for all objects. You create class variables with the `static` keyword.

Class variables are often useful: for example, you can use a class variable to keep track of the number of objects of a particular class created in a program. You'll do that in this task.

To use class variables:

1. Create a new program named **classvariables.m**.
2. In classvariables.m, enter the code shown in **Listing 6.7**.

   This code creates a class with a class variable named `count`.

continues on next page

3. Add the code to create two objects and display the object count each time (**Listing 6.8**).
4. Save classvariables.m.
5. Run the classvariables.m program.

   You should see the following:

   ```
   TheClass count is 1
   TheClass count is 2
   ```

```
#import <stdio.h>
#import <Foundation/NSObject.h>

@interface TheClass: NSObject
static int count;
+(int) getCount;
@end

@implementation TheClass
-(TheClass*) init
{
    self = [super init];
    count++;
    return self;
}

+(int) getCount
{
    return count;
}
@end

int main(void)
{
  TheClass *tc1 = [TheClass new];

  printf( "TheClass count is %i\n",
    [TheClass getCount] );

  TheClass *tc2 = [TheClass new];

  printf( "TheClass count is %i\n",
    [TheClass getCount] );

  return 0;
}
```

Listing 6.8 The classvariables.m program.

```
#import <stdio.h>
#import <Foundation/NSObject.h>

@interface TheClass: NSObject
static int count;
+(int) getCount;
@end

@implementation TheClass
-(TheClass*) init
{
    self = [super init];
    count++;
        .
        .
        .
}

+(int) getCount
{
    return count;
}
@end

int main(void)
{
  TheClass *tc1 = [TheClass new];

  printf( "TheClass count is %i\n",
    [TheClass getCount] );

  TheClass *tc2 = [TheClass new];

  printf( "TheClass count is %i\n",
    [TheClass getCount] );

  return 0;
}
```

Listing 6.9 Editing classvariables.m.

Accessing the Current Object

Sometimes, you need to access the current object while executing code in that object. For example, from constructors you need to return a pointer to the current object after you've finished configuring it.

To get a pointer to the current object, use the `self` keyword. You've seen self before, but it deserves its own task.

To access the current object:

1. Open the classvariables.m program from the previous task for editing.
2. Assign the pointer returned by the base class's constructor to the `self` pointer (**Listing 6.9**).

continued on next page

3. Use the `self` keyword to get a pointer to the current object (**Listing 6.10**).

Here, you're returning a pointer to the current object from the constructor.

```
#import <stdio.h>
#import <Foundation/NSObject.h>

@interface TheClass: NSObject
static int count;
+(int) getCount;
@end

@implementation TheClass
-(TheClass*) init
{
    self = [super init];
    count++;
    return self;
}

+(int) getCount
{
    return count;
}
@end

int main(void)
{
  TheClass *tc1 = [TheClass new];

  printf( "TheClass count is %i\n",
    [TheClass getCount] );

  TheClass *tc2 = [TheClass new];

  printf( "TheClass count is %i\n",
    [TheClass getCount] );

  return 0;
}
```

Listing 6.10 The classvariables.m program with a pointer to the current object.

```
#import <stdio.h>
#include <Foundation/Foundation.h>

@interface Class1: NSObject
-(void) print;
@end

@implementation Class1
-(void) print
{
    printf("This is Class 1.\n");
}
@end

@interface Class2: NSObject
-(void) print;
@end

@implementation Class2
-(void) print
{
    printf("This is Class 2.\n");
}
@end
        .
        .
        .
```

Listing 6.11 Starting id.m.

Creating a Variable for Multiple Object Types

In Objective-C, the `id` type can stand for any type of object. That's useful when you have one variable that you want to contain multiple types of objects.

In this task, you create objects of two different class types and place them in the same variable of type `id`.

To use the id type:

1. Create a new program named **id.m**.
2. In id.m, enter the code shown in **Listing 6.11**.

   This code creates the two classes you'll use.

continues on next page

3. Add the code to create two objects of different classes and store those objects, one after the other, in the `id` variable (**Listing 6.12**).
4. Save id.m.
5. Run the id.m program.

   You should see the following:

   ```
   This is Class 1.
   This is Class 2.
   ```

```
#import <stdio.h>
#include <Foundation/Foundation.h>

@interface Class1: NSObject
-(void) print;
@end

@implementation Class1
-(void) print
{
   printf("This is Class 1.\n");
}
@end

@interface Class2: NSObject
-(void) print;
@end

@implementation Class2
-(void) print
{
   printf("This is Class 2.\n");
}
@end

int main(void)
{
   Class1 *c1 = [Class1 new];
   Class2 *c2 = [Class2 new];
   id container;

   container = c1;
   [container print];

   container = c2;
   [container print];

   return 0;
}
```

Listing 6.12 The id.m program.

```
#import <stdio.h>
#include <Foundation/Foundation.h>

@interface Class1: NSObject
-(void) print;
@end

@implementation Class1
-(void) print
{
    printf("This is Class 1.\n");
}
@end
        .
        .
        .
```

Listing 6.13 Starting isMemberOfClass.m.

Verifying That an Object Belongs to a Class

You can determine whether an object is a member of a certain class with the `isMemberOfClass` method. You'll put that method to use in the next task to verify that a certain object is a member of a certain class, here called `Class1`. You can get the class's name simply by sending it the message `class` like this: `[Class1 class]`.

To use isMemberOfClass:

1. Create a new program named **isMemberOfClass.m**.
2. In isMemberOfClass.m, enter the code shown in **Listing 6.13**.

   This code creates the `Class1` class.

continues on next page

3. Add the code to create an object of the `Class1` class and verify that the object really is a member of the `Class1` class (**Listing 6.14**).
4. Save isMemberOfClass.m.
5. Run the isMemberOfClass.m program. You should see the following:

   `c1 is a member of Class1.`

```
#import <stdio.h>
#include <Foundation/Foundation.h>

@interface Class1: NSObject
-(void) print;
@end

@implementation Class1
-(void) print
{
    printf("This is Class 1.\n");
}
@end

int main(void)
{
  Class1 *c1 = [Class1 new];

  if ( [c1 isMemberOfClass: [Class1
    class]] == YES )
  {
    printf("c1 is a member of Class1.\n" );
  }

  return 0;
}
```

Listing 6.14 The isMemberOfClass.m program.

```
#import <stdio.h>
#include <Foundation/Foundation.h>

@interface Class1: NSObject
-(void) print;
@end

@implementation Class1
-(void) print
{
    printf("This is Class 1.\n");
}
@end
        .
        .
        .
```

Listing 6.15 Starting isKindOfClass.m.

Checking an Object's Class with isKindOfClass

You can also use `isKindOfClass` to determine whether an object is a member of a class. What is the difference between `isMemberOfClass` and `isKindOfClass`? You can use `isKindOfClass` to determine whether an object is a member of a class—or of any class derived from that class.

For example, we've been deriving our classes from the `NSObject` class, and while `isMemberOfClass` wouldn't detect that fact for any class we've based on `NSObject`, `isKindOfClass` would.

✔ Tip

- See Chapter 7 for all the details on deriving one class from another.

To use isKindOfClass:

1. Create a new program named **isKindOfClass.m**.
2. In isKindOfClass.m, enter the code shown in **Listing 6.15**.

   This code creates the `Class1` class, which is based on the `NSObject` class.

continues on next page

3. Add the code to use `isKindOfClass` to determine whether `Class1` is a kind of `NSObject` class (**Listing 6.16**).

4. Save isKindOfClass.m.

5. Run the isKindOfClass.m program. You should see the following:
   `c1 is a kind of NSObject.`

```
#import <stdio.h>
#include <Foundation/Foundation.h>

@interface Class1: NSObject
-(void) print;
@end

@implementation Class1
-(void) print
{
    printf("This is Class 1.\n");
}
@end

int main(void)
{
  Class1 *c1 = [Class1 new];

  if ( [c1 isKindOfClass: [NSObject
    class]] == YES )
  {
  printf("c1 is a kind of NSObject.\n" );
  }

  return 0;
}
```

Listing 6.16 The isKindOfClass.m program.

```
#import <stdio.h>
#include <Foundation/Foundation.h>

@interface Class1: NSObject
-(void) print;
@end

@implementation Class1
-(void) print
{
    printf("This is Class 1.\n");
}
@end
        .
        .
        .
```

Listing 6.17 Starting responds.m.

```
#import <stdio.h>
#include <Foundation/Foundation.h>

@interface Class1: NSObject
-(void) print;
@end

@implementation Class1
-(void) print
{
    printf("This is Class 1.\n");
}
@end

int main(void)
{
  Class1 *c1 = [Class1 new];

  if ([c1 respondsToSelector:
    @selector(print)] == YES ) {
    printf("c1 has a print method.\n");
  }

  return 0;
}
```

Listing 6.18 The responds.m program.

Verifying That an Object Supports a Method

In Objective-C, objects can support methods. But how do you know if a particular object supports a particular method? To check whether an object supports a method, you can use the `respondsToSelector()`function.

To check whether an object will respond to a specific message:

1. Create a new program named **responds.m**.
2. In responds.m, enter the code shown in **Listing 6.17**.

   This code creates the `Class1` class that has a method named `print`.
3. Enter the code to check whether an object of `Class1` supports a method named `print` (**Listing 6.18**).
4. Save responds.m.
5. Run the responds.m program.

   You should see the following:

   `c1 has a print method.`

Checking Whether Objects Support a Method

Besides checking whether an object supports a particular method, you can check whether a class will create objects that support a particular method. To do that, you use the `instancesRespondToSelector` method.

To verify that a class creates objects that support a particular method:

1. Create a new program named **instances.m**.
2. In instances.m, enter the code shown in **Listing 6.19**.

   This code creates the `Class1` class that supports the `print` method.
3. Add the code to check whether objects created from the `Class1` class will support the `print` method (**Listing 6.20**).
4. Save instances.m.
5. Run the instances.m program.

   You should see the following:

   `Class1 objects have a print method`

```
#import <stdio.h>
#include <Foundation/Foundation.h>

@interface Class1: NSObject
-(void) print;
@end

@implementation Class1
-(void) print
{
    printf("This is Class 1.\n");
}
@end
         .
         .
         .
```

Listing 6.19 Starting instances.m.

```
#import <stdio.h>
#include <Foundation/Foundation.h>

@interface Class1: NSObject
-(void) print;
@end

@implementation Class1
-(void) print
{
    printf("This is Class 1.\n");
}
@end

int main(void)
{
  if ([Class1 instancesRespondToSelector:
    @selector(print)] == YES ) {
    printf(
  "Class1 objects have a print method\n"
    );
  }

  return 0;
}
```

Listing 6.20 The instances.m program.

Working with Object-Oriented Inheritance

7

This chapter discusses the process of deriving one class from another—a process called *inheritance*.

You can derive one class from another in Objective-C. The class you derive from is called the *base class*, and the new class you're deriving from the base class is called the *derived class*.

The derived class can inherit all the functionality of the base class, and it can customize that functionality as well. For example, you might have a base class named `Animal` that creates a generic animal. The `Animal` class might have a method to set the animal's name, `setName`, and another to get the animal's name, `getName`. Then, no matter what kind of animal you want to create, `Animal` can serve as a base class for it, and all the derived animals will have built-in `setName` and `getName` methods.

You might use `Animal` as a base class for other classes, such as `Cat` and `Dog`. If you create a class named `Cat`, for example, you might want more than just `setName` and `getName` methods; for instance, you might also want add your own method, the `meow` method, which prints out "Meow."

continues on next page

If you also derive a class named Dog from the Animal class, you might add a method named bark to it.

The Cat class would then have the methods setName, getName, and meow. The Dog class would have the methods setName, getName, and bark. So as you can see, although the Dog and Cat classes share some functionality, because they are both classes of animals, they also have been customized.

That's the idea behind inheritance: you use inheritance when you want to create classes that share some functionality. Using inheritance, you can save a lot of work. In this example, in addition to the Cat and Dog classes, you might use the Animal class to derive the Tiger, Leopard, Lion, Squid, and Ocelot classes.

You can also have multi-level inheritance. So, for example, you might use the Dog class as the base class for the Terrier and Collie classes.

✔ Tip

- Although inheritance in Objective-C is a powerful tool, it lacks some capabilities found in C++ and some other object-oriented programming languages. For instance, it lacks operator overloading and also multiple inheritance (in which a single class can inherit from multiple other classes).

```
#import <stdio.h>
#include <Foundation/Foundation.h>

@interface Class1: NSObject
@end

@implementation Class1
@end

@interface Class2: Class1
@end

@implementation Class2
@end
        .
        .
        .
```

Listing 7.1 Creating inheritance.m.

```
#import <stdio.h>
#include <Foundation/Foundation.h>

@interface Class1: NSObject
@end

@implementation Class1
@end

@interface Class2: Class1
@end

@implementation Class2
@end

int main(void)
{
  printf("The inheritance worked.\n");

  return 0;
}
```

Listing 7.2 The access.m program.

Inheriting from a Class

We'll start by taking a look at how to inherit one class from another. In fact, the programs you've been working with have already been inheriting classes from `NSObject`, and extending that capability to any class is easy.

Here, you'll create one class, `Class1`, based on `NSObject`:

```
@interface Class1: NSObject
@end
```

Then you'll create another class, `Class2`, based on `Class1`:

```
@interface Class2: Class1
@end
```

These classes won't actually do anything—we're just looking at the syntax of inheritance at this point. In the subsequent tasks, you'll add data members and methods to base and derived classes.

To inherit from a class:

1. Create a new program file named **inheritance.m**.
2. In inheritance.m, enter the code shown in **Listing 7.1** to create `Class1` and base `Class2` on it.
3. Display a message in the `main()` function to indicate that the inheritance worked (**Listing 7.2**).
4. Save inheritance.m.
5. Run the inheritance.m program.
   You should see the following:
   `The inheritance worked.`

Inheriting Base-Class Data Members

When you base one class on another, all data members not declared as `@private` are accessible in the derived class.

In this example, you'll declare a data member named `data` in the base class and reference it from an object of the derived class.

To inherit base-class data members:

1. Create a program named **inheritdata.m**.
2. In inheritdata.m, enter the new code highlighted in **Listing 7.3**.

   This code creates `Class1` with a data member named `data` and derives a class named `Class2` based on it. Note that the data member is declared `@public`, which makes it accessible from code in the base class, the derived class, and any other code in the program.

```
#import <stdio.h>
#include <Foundation/Foundation.h>

@interface Class1: NSObject
{
@public
  int data;
}
@end

@implementation Class1
@end

@interface Class2: Class1
@end

@implementation Class2
@end
        .
        .
        .
```

Listing 7.3 Starting inheritdata.m.

```
#import <stdio.h>
#include <Foundation/Foundation.h>

@interface Class1: NSObject
{
@public
  int data;
}
@end

@implementation Class1
@end

@interface Class2: Class1
@end

@implementation Class2
@end

int main(void)
{
  Class2 *c2 = [Class2 new];
  c2->data = 5;

  printf("The data is %i.\n", c2->data);

  return 0;
}
```

Listing 7.4 The inheritdata.m program.

3. Add code to create an object of the derived class, `Class2`, and access the data member using that object (**Listing 7.4**).
4. Save inheritdata.m.
5. Run the inheritance.m program.
   You should see the following:
   `The data is 5.`

Inheriting Base-Class Methods

When a derived class inherits a base class, the methods of the base class are available to you in the derived class unless they're marked `@private`.

In this task, a derived class will inherit a base class that has one method, and the derived class will add a new method. Then you'll call both methods to verify that they work as they should.

To inherit base-class methods:

1. Create a program named **inheritmethods.m**.
2. In inheritmethods.m, enter the new code highlighted in **Listing 7.5**.

   This code creates `Class1` and `Class2`, each with a built-in method..

```
#import <stdio.h>
#include <Foundation/Foundation.h>

@interface Class1: NSObject
-(void) print;
@end

@implementation Class1
-(void) print
{
    printf("This is Class 1.\n");
}
@end

@interface Class2: Class1
-(void) print2;
@end

@implementation Class2
-(void) print2
{
    printf("This is Class 2.\n");
}
@end
        .
        .
        .
```

Listing 7.5 Starting inheritmethods.m.

```
#import <stdio.h>
#include <Foundation/Foundation.h>

@interface Class1: NSObject
-(void) print;
@end

@implementation Class1
-(void) print
{
   printf("This is Class 1.\n");
}
@end

@interface Class2: Class1
-(void) print2;
@end

@implementation Class2
-(void) print2
{
   printf("This is Class 2.\n");
}
@end

int main(void)
{
   Class2 *c2 = [Class2 new];

   [c2 print];
   [c2 print2];

   return 0;
}
```

Listing 7.6 The inheritmethods.m program.

3. Add the code to create an object of the derived class and call both the base class method and the derived class method to verify that they work (**Listing 7.6**)
4. Save inheritmethods.m.
5. Run the inheritmethods.m program.

   You should see the following:

   ```
   This is Class 1.
   This is Class 2.
   ```

Overriding Base-Class Methods

Say that you have a method in a base class that you need to change. For example, say you have a method named `print` in the base class `Class1` that prints "This is class 1." Clearly, in the derived class, `Class2`, the message should say, "This is class 2."

You can *override* the base class `print` method just by redefining it in the derived class. When you override a method in a derived class, the overriding method must have the same prototype (same return type and arguments) as the method you're overriding.

To override base-class methods:

1. Create a new program named **override.m**.
2. In override.m, enter the code shown in **Listing 7.7**.

   This code creates `Class1` and derives `Class2` from it. Each class has a method named `print` with the same prototype, so the `Class2` version will override the `Class1` version.

```
#import <stdio.h>
#include <Foundation/Foundation.h>

@interface Class1: NSObject
-(void) print;
@end

@implementation Class1
-(void) print
{
  printf("This is Class 1.\n");
}
@end

@interface Class2: Class1
-(void) print;
@end

@implementation Class2
-(void) print
{
  printf("This is Class 2.\n");
}
@end
        .
        .
        .
```

Listing 7.7 Starting override.m.

```
#import <stdio.h>
#include <Foundation/Foundation.h>

@interface Class1: NSObject
-(void) print;
@end

@implementation Class1
-(void) print
{
  printf("This is Class 1.\n");
}
@end

@interface Class2: Class1
-(void) print;
@end

@implementation Class2
-(void) print
{
  printf("This is Class 2.\n");
}
@end

int main(void)
{
  Class2 *c2 = [Class2 new];

  [c2 print];

  return 0;
}
```

Listing 7.8 The override.m program.

3. Add the code to create an object of `Class2` and call the overridden `print` method (**Listing 7.8**).
4. Save override.m.
5. Run the override.m program.
   You should see the following:
   `This is Class 2.`

Overloading Base-Class Methods

You can also *overload* methods. When you overload a method, you give it multiple definitions, and Objective-C chooses the correct version of the method based on the parameter list—the type and number of parameters must be different for each version of an overloaded method.

To overload a base-class method:

1. Create a new program named **overload.m**.
2. In overload.m, enter the code shown in **Listing 7.9**.

   This code creates `Class1` and derives `Class2` from it; `Class1` has a `print` method with no arguments, and `Class2` has a `print` method that takes one argument.

```
#import <stdio.h>
#include <Foundation/Foundation.h>

@interface Class1: NSObject
-(void) print;
@end

@implementation Class1
-(void) print
{
    printf("Hello there.\n");
}
@end

@interface Class2: Class1
-(void) print: (int) x;
@end

@implementation Class2
-(void) print: (int) x
{
  printf("Your number is %i.\n", x);
}
@end


int main(void)
{
  Class2 *c2 = [Class2 new];

  [c2 print];
  [c2 print: 5];

  return 0;
}
        .
        .
        .
```

Listing 7.9 Starting overload.m.

```
#import <stdio.h>
#include <Foundation/Foundation.h>

@interface Class1: NSObject
-(void) print;
@end

@implementation Class1
-(void) print
{
   printf("Hello there.\n");
}
@end

@interface Class2: Class1
-(void) print: (int) x;
@end

@implementation Class2
-(void) print: (int) x
{
  printf("Your number is %i.\n", x);
}
@end

int main(void)
{
  Class2 *c2 = [Class2 new];

  [c2 print];
  [c2 print: 5];

  return 0;
}
```

Listing 7.10 The overload.m program.

3. Add the code to create an object of `Class2` and call the two `print` methods: one with an argument. and one without (**Listing 7.10**).
4. Save overload.m.
5. Run the overload.m program.

   You should see the following:

   ```
   Hello there.
   Your number is 5.
   ```

Using Multi-level Inheritance

Inheritance in Objective-C isn't limited to a single level. Classes can inherit as many levels of base classes as you want. The example in this task shows two-level inheritance.

To use multi-level inheritance:

1. Create a new program named **multilevel.m**.
2. In multilevel.m, enter the code shown in **Listing 7.11**.

   This code creates the three classes you'll use.

```
#import <stdio.h>
#include <Foundation/Foundation.h>
@interface Class1: NSObject
-(void) print;
@end
@implementation Class1
-(void) print
{
   printf("This is Class 1.\n");
}
@end
@interface Class2: Class1
-(void) print2;
@end
@implementation Class2
-(void) print2
{
   printf("This is Class 2.\n");
}
@end
@interface Class3: Class2
-(void) print3;
@end
@implementation Class3
-(void) print3
{
   printf("This is Class 3.\n");
}
@end
      .
      .
      .
```

Listing 7.11 Starting multilevel.m.

```
#import <stdio.h>
#include <Foundation/Foundation.h>

@interface Class1: NSObject
-(void) print;
@end

@implementation Class1
-(void) print
{
   printf("This is Class 1.\n");
}
@end

@interface Class2: Class1
-(void) print2;
@end

@implementation Class2
-(void) print2
{
   printf("This is Class 2.\n");
}
@end

@interface Class3: Class2
-(void) print3;
@end

@implementation Class3
-(void) print3
{
   printf("This is Class 3.\n");
}
@end

int main(void)
{
   Class3 *c3 = [Class3 new];

   [c3 print];
   [c3 print2];
   [c3 print3];

   return 0;
}
```

Listing 7.12 The multilevel.m program.

3. Add the code to create two objects of the different classes and store those objects, one after the other, in the `id` variable (**Listing 7.12**).

4. Save multilevel.m.

5. Run the multilevel.m program.

   You should see the following:

   ```
   This is Class 1.
   This is Class 2.
   This is Class 3..
   ```

Limiting Access

By default, the data members and methods of a base class are available to code in the derived class. That may not always be a good idea, however: for example, if the base class has an internal variable that keeps track of some count that the derived class doesn't need access to. In such cases, you can use the `@private` access specifier to mark such a data member as private. You saw `@private` in the previous chapter, but here you'll use it with inheritance.

To stop inheritance:

1. Create a new program named **private.m**.
2. In private.m, enter the code shown in **Listing 7.13**.

   This code creates the classes you'll use and marks a data member of the base class as private.

```
#import <stdio.h>
#import <Foundation/NSObject.h>

@interface Class1: NSObject {
@private
    int privateVariable;
}
@end

@implementation Class1
@end

@interface Class2: Class1
-(void) print;
@end

@implementation Class2
-(void) print
{
        .
        .
        .
}
@end
        .
        .
        .
```

Listing 7.13 Starting private.m.

```
#import <stdio.h>
#import <Foundation/NSObject.h>

@interface Class1: NSObject {
@private
    int privateVariable;
}
@end

@implementation Class1
@end

@interface Class2: Class1
-(void) print;
@end

@implementation Class2
-(void) print
{
  privateVariable = 5;
  printf("The private variable is %i.",
    privateVariable);
}
@end

int main(void)
{
  Class2 *c = [Class2 new];

  [c print];

  return 0;
}
```

Listing 7.14 The private.m program.

3. Add the code to try to access the private variable of the base class using code in the derived class (**Listing 7.14**).
4. Save private.m.
5. Try to run the private.m program.

   Depending on your platform, you'll either get a hard error (the program will not compile) or a warning with a message that, in the future, the warning will be a hard error.

Restricting Access

You can also restrict inheritance if you mark class members with `@protected`. This access specifier is less restrictive than `@private`; derived classes can still use the protected members of the base class, but no other code can. That is, protected members are available only to the code in the base class and any classes derived from the base class. You learned about `@protected` in the previous chapter; here, you'll use it with inheritance.

To restrict inheritance:

1. Create a new program named **protected.m**.
2. In protected.m, enter the code shown in **Listing 7.15**.

   This code creates the two classes you'll use.

```
#import <stdio.h>
#import <Foundation/NSObject.h>

@interface Class1: NSObject {
@protected
    int protectedVariable;
}
@end

@implementation Class1
@end

@interface Class2: Class1
-(void) print;
@end

@implementation Class2
-(void) print
{
        .
        .
        .
}
@end
        .
        .
        .
```

Listing 7.15 Starting protected.m.

```
#import <stdio.h>
#import <Foundation/NSObject.h>

@interface Class1: NSObject {
@protected
    int protectedVariable;
}
@end

@implementation Class1
@end

@interface Class2: Class1
-(void) print;
@end

@implementation Class2
-(void) print
{
  protectedVariable = 5;
  printf("The protected variable is %i.",
    protectedVariable);
}
@end

int main(void)
{
  Class2 *c = [Class2 new];

  [c print];

  return 0;
}
```

Listing 7.16 The protected.m program.

3. Add the code to access the protected data member in the derived class (**Listing 7.16**).
4. Save protected.m.
5. Run the protected.m program.

   You should see the following:

   `The protected variable is 5.`

Using Constructors with Inheritance

What if the base class has a constructor? You can call a base class's constructor, passing to it any arguments you want, when you use the `super` keyword. The `super` keyword allows you to access the base class in your code

In this task, you'll access the base class's constructor.

✔ Tip

- *Super* refers to superclass, another word for the base class.

To use constructors with inheritance:

1. Create a new program named **constructor.m**.
2. In constructor.m, enter the code shown in **Listing 7.17**.

   This code creates the `Class1` class that has a constructor named `init` that uses the `super` keyword.

```
#import <stdio.h>
#import <Foundation/NSObject.h>
@interface TheClass: NSObject
static int count;
+(int) getCount;
@end

@implementation TheClass
-(TheClass*) init
{
    self = [super init];
    count++;
    return self;
}

+(int) getCount
{
    return count;
}
@end

int main(void)
{
  TheClass *tc1 = [TheClass new];

  printf( "TheClass count is %i\n",
    [TheClass getCount] );

  TheClass *tc2 = [TheClass new];

  printf( "TheClass count is %i\n",
    [TheClass getCount] );

  return 0;
}
        .
        .
        .
```

Listing 7.17 Starting constructor.m.

```
#import <stdio.h>
#import <Foundation/NSObject.h>

@interface TheClass: NSObject
static int count;
+(int) getCount;
@end

@implementation TheClass
-(TheClass*) init
{
    self = [super init];
    count++;
    return self;
}

+(int) getCount
{
    return count;
}
@end

int main(void)
{
  TheClass *tc1 = [TheClass new];

  printf( "TheClass count is %i\n",
    [TheClass getCount] );

  TheClass *tc2 = [TheClass new];

  printf( "TheClass count is %i\n",
    [TheClass getCount] );

  return 0;
}
```

Listing 7.18 The constructor.m program.

3. Enter the code to create an object of `Class1`, which will call the constructor (**Listing 7.18**).
4. Save constructor.m.
5. Run the constructor.m program. You should see the following:

```
TheClass count is 1
TheClass count is 2
```

Using Polymorphism

Polymorphism refers to using the same code with different objects: that is, when you use polymorphism, the actual object that is used when you pass it a message is determined at run time.

For example, in this task, you'll execute the same code twice:

```
[pointerToObject print];
```

The `pointerToObject` variable will hold a pointer to a different object each time the code is executed, so the object to which the message is sent is determined when the code runs.

To use polymorphism:

1. Create a new program named **polymorphism.m**.
2. In polymorphism.m, enter the code shown in **Listing 7.19**.

   This code creates the two classes you'll use.

```
#import <stdio.h>
#include <Foundation/Foundation.h>
@interface Class1: NSObject
-(void) print;
@end
@implementation Class1
-(void) print
{
   printf("This is Class 1.\n");
}
@end
@interface Class2: NSObject
-(void) print;
@end
@implementation Class2
-(void) print
{
   printf("This is Class 2.\n");
}
@end
      .
      .
      .
```

Listing 7.19 Starting polymorphism.m.

```
#import <stdio.h>
#include <Foundation/Foundation.h>

@interface Class1: NSObject
-(void) print;
@end

@implementation Class1
-(void) print
{
   printf("This is Class 1.\n");
}
@end

@interface Class2: NSObject
-(void) print;
@end

@implementation Class2
-(void) print
{
   printf("This is Class 2.\n");
}
@end

int main(void)
{
  Class1 *c1 = [Class1 new];
  Class2 *c2 = [Class2 new];
  id pointerToObject;
  int loopIndex;

  pointerToObject = c1;

  for(loopIndex = 0; loopIndex < 2;
    loopIndex++){

    [pointerToObject print];

    pointerToObject = c2;
  }

  return 0;}
```

Listing 7.20 The polymorphism.m program.

3. Add the code to load a variable of the `id` type with pointers to the two objects, one after the other, and execute the same line of code for each object (**Listing 7.20**).
4. Save polymorphism.m.
5. Run the polymorphism.m program.
   You should see the following:
   `This is Class 1.`
   `This is Class 2.`

Categories, Posing, and Protocols

In this chapter, we're going look at three features of Objective-C object-oriented programming: categories, posing, and protocols.

Categories let you extend a class by adding methods to a class—and you don't need access to the base class's code to do it; you can create new methods for a class without editing the class's definition in code. That can be useful when you don't have access to the source code for a class, or when you don't want to change the source code, or when you want to customize a class in different ways.

To use categories, you create a new file with the interfaces for the new methods, use Objective-C syntax to indicate that you're extending another class, and then put the implementations of the new methods in another file. "Categories" is the actual name of the new methods you add to the class.

Posing involves making one class "pose" as another. Say that you have a class, `Class1`, and another class, `Class2`, derived from `Class1`. You can create objects of `Class1`, of course. But you can also tell `Class2` to pose as `Class1`. From then on in your code, whenever you create an object of `Class1`, you'll really be creating an object of `Class2`. In other words, `Class2` is posing as `Class1`.

continues on next page

There are other ways of doing the same thing—you could use polymorphism, for example (see the previous chapter). But using posing can be cleaner because you don't have to keep track of what kind of pointer is stored in your variables all the way through your code.

Protocols are much like what are called interfaces in Java. A protocol is a specification for a method, much like its prototype. When you indicate that a certain class uses specific protocols, you're indicating that that class implements those methods. In other words, protocols let you declare methods; it's up to you to define the implementation in your class.

This is the closest Objective-C comes to multiple inheritance, in which you inherit from multiple classes, because using protocols, you can make sure all your derived classes implement the same methods (although the actual implementation in each class may be different). That's useful if, for example, you have two base classes, named `Animal` and `Pet`, and want to derive classes named `Cat` and `Dog` from them. You can make sure that `Cat` and `Dog` implement the methods of `Animal` and `Pet` by using protocols. When `Cat` and `Dog` use the protocols defined by `Animal` and `Pet`, `Cat` and `Dog` both automatically implement a list of methods.

About Categories

Categories let you extend a class by defining new methods, even if you don't have access to that class's source code or can't change it.

Say you have a class, `Class1`, with a single method, `method1`, in the class's header file:

```
#include <Foundation/Foundation.h>

@interface Class1: NSObject
-(return_type) method1;
@end
```

Suppose also that the method is defined in the class's implementation file:

```
#import <stdio.h>
#include <Foundation/Foundation.h>

@implementation Class1
-(return_type) method1
{
        .
        .
        .
}
@end
```

If you want to extend `Class1` by adding a new method, `method2`, you can create a new header file that lists the `method2` interface, like this:

```
@interface Class1 (Extender)
-(return_type) method2;
@end
```

continues on next page

Note the term Extender in parentheses after the class name. You can use whatever term you want here to indicate that you're extending the base class and to give a name to that extension. You use the same term in parentheses when you create the implementation of method2 in its own file:

```
#import <stdio.h>
#include <Foundation/Foundation.h>

@implementation Class1 (Extender)
-(return_type) method2
{
        .
        .
        .
}
@end
```

In this way, Objective-C allows you to extend classes without modifying their source code files.

```
#import <stdio.h>
#include <Foundation/Foundation.h>
#import "Class1.h"

@implementation Class1
        .
        .
        .
@end
```

Listing 8.1 Starting class1.m.

```
#import <stdio.h>
#include <Foundation/Foundation.h>
#import "Class1.h"

@implementation Class1
-(void) print
{
   printf("This is Class 1.\n");
}
@end
```

Listing 8.2 The class1.m program.

```
#include <Foundation/Foundation.h>

@interface Class1: NSObject
-(void) print;
@end
```

Listing 8.3 The class1.h file.

Categories: Creating the Base Class

In this task, you'll create a base class that you'll extend in the next task using categories. You'll create a class named `Class1` that contains a method named `print`. Here's what the `print` method looks like; it just prints the message "This is Class 1."

```
-(void) print
{
   printf("This is Class 1.\n");
}
```

To create the base class that will be extended:

1. Create a program named **class1.m**.
2. In class1.m, enter the code in **Listing 8.1**.
   This code creates the `Class1` class.
3. In class1.m, add the code to create the `print` method (**Listing 8.2**).
4. Save class1.m.
5. Create a header file named **class1.h**.
6. In class1.h, enter the code shown in **Listing 8.3**.
7. Save class1.h.
   Now you're ready to extend the class.

Categories: Creating Categories

In the preceding task, you created `Class1`, complete with a `print` method. In the task here, you'll extend `Class1` using categories to include a new method, `print2`.

The `print2` method looks like this:

```
-(void) print2
{
   printf(
   "This is Class 1 extended.\n");
}
```

After adding this method to `Class1`, you'll call both methods, `method1` and `method2`, in the next task.

To add categories to a class:

1. Create a program named **class1extender.m**.
2. In class1extender.m, enter the code in **Listing 8.4**.

   This code indicates that you want to extend `Class1` using categories.
3. In class1extender.m, add the code to create the `print2` method (**Listing 8.5**).
4. Save class1extender.m.
5. Create a file named **class1extender.h**.
6. In class1.h, enter the code in **Listing 8.6**.
7. Save class1extender.h.

```
#import <stdio.h>
#include <Foundation/Foundation.h>
#import "Class1.h"
#import "Class1extender.h"

@implementation Class1 (Extender)
      .
      .
      .
@end
```

Listing 8.4 Starting class1extender.m.

```
#import <stdio.h>
#include <Foundation/Foundation.h>
#import "Class1.h"
#import "Class1extender.h"

@implementation Class1 (Extender)
-(void) print2
{
   printf(
   "This is Class 1 extended.\n");
}
@end
```

Listing 8.5 The class1extender.m program.

```
@interface Class1 (Extender)
-(void) print2;
@end
```

Listing 8.6 The class1extender.h file.

```
#import <stdio.h>
#import "Class1.h"
#import "Class1extender.h"

int main(void)
{
        .
        .
        .
}
```

Listing 8.7 Starting main.m.

```
#import <stdio.h>
#import "Class1.h"
#import "Class1extender.h"

int main(void)
{
    Class1 *c1 = [Class1 new];
        .
        .
        .
}
```

Listing 8.8 Editing main.m.

Categories: Putting It All Together

In the previous two tasks, you created `Class1` and extended it using categories. In this task, you'll put the `Class1` class and its extension category to work.

To use the base class with categories:

1. Create a new program named **main.m**.
2. In main.m, enter the code shown in **Listing 8.7**.

   This code includes the class1.h and class1extender.h header files to make sure your code knows about `Class1` and its extending categories.
3. In main.m, add the code to create a new object of `Class1` (**Listing 8.8**).

continues on next page

4. In main.m, add the code shown in **Listing 8.9**.

   This code calls the `print` method built into the `Class1` class and the `print2` method with which you've extended `Class1`.

5. Save main.m.

6. If you're using Linux, UNIX, or Windows, create a new makefile named **GNUmakefile**.

7. In GNUmakefile, enter the code shown in **Listing 8.10**.

8. Save GNUmakefile.

9. Run the main.m categories program.

   You should see the output from both the `print` method and the extending `print2` method:

   ```
   This is Class 1.
   This is Class 1 extended.
   ```

```
#import <stdio.h>
#import "Class1.h"
#import "Class1extender.h"
#import "FractionMath.h"

int main(void)
{
    Class1 *c1 = [Class1 new];

    [c1 print];
    [c1 print2];

    return 0;
}
```

Listing 8.9 Calling the print and print2 methods.

```
include $(GNUSTEP_MAKEFILES)/common.make

TOOL_NAME = categories
categories_OBJC_FILES = Class1.m
Class1extender.m main.m

include $(GNUSTEP_MAKEFILES)/tool.make
```

Listing 8.10 GNUmakefile.

About Posing

Posing lets one class stand in for another. Say you have a class, `Class1`, with a single method, `method1`, in the class's header file:

```
#include <Foundation/Foundation.h>

@interface Class1: NSObject
-(return_type) method1;
@end
```

Suppose also that the method is defined in the class's implementation file:

```
#import <stdio.h>
#include <Foundation/Foundation.h>

@implementation Class1
-(return_type) method1
{
        .
        .
        .
}
@end
```

Now say that the method is redefined in another class's implementation file, and that `Class2` is based on `Class1`:

```
#import <stdio.h>
#include <Foundation/Foundation.h>

@implementation Class1 : Class2
-(return_type) method1
{
        .
        .
        .
}
@end
```

continues on next page

You can have Class2 pose as Class1 in your main method like this:

```
[Class2 poseAsClass: [Class1 class]];
```

Now when you create an object of Class1, like this:

```
Class1 *c2 = [Class1 new];

[c2 method1];
        .
        .
        .
```

you're really creating an object of Class2. The method that will be run in this code is the method1 defined in the Class2 implementation.

This technique is useful as a shortcut way of handling polymorphism, but you have to remember that you're having one class pose as another when you're writing the code that follows the poseAsClass line.

```
#import <stdio.h>
#include <Foundation/Foundation.h>
#import "Class1.h"

@implementation Class1
        .
        .
        .
@end
```

Listing 8.11 Starting class1.m.

```
#import <stdio.h>
#include <Foundation/Foundation.h>
#import "Class1.h"

@implementation Class1
-(void) print
{
   printf("This is Class 1.\n");
}
@end
```

Listing 8.12 The class1.m program.

```
#include <Foundation/Foundation.h>

@interface Class1: NSObject
-(void) print;
@end
```

Listing 8.13 The class1.h file.

Posing: Creating the Base Class

When a class poses as another class, it can function as a stand-in for that class. You tell Objective-C that one class is posing for another, and from then on in your code, Objective-C uses the class that's posing as the original class, even when you use the original class in your code.

To create the base class for which another class can pose:

1. Create a file named **class1.m**.
2. In class1.m, enter the code in **Listing 8.11**.
   This code creates the `Class1` class.
3. In class1.m, add the code to create the `print` method (**Listing 8.12**).
4. Save class1.m.
5. Create a file named **class1.h**.
6. In class1.h, enter the code in **Listing 8.13**.
7. Save class1.h.

Posing: Creating the Derived Class

One class can pose as another only if it's based on the class it's posing as, so in this task, you'll derive a class from the base class, `Class1`. This new class will be called `Class2`, and it will redefine the `print` method to display a message indicating that this is `Class2`:

```
@implementation Class2
-(void) print
{
   printf("This is Class 2.\n");
}
```

This way, when `Class2` poses as `Class1` and you call the `print` method, you'll see the message "This is Class 2.", not "This is Class 1."

To create the derived class:

1. Create a file named **class2.m**.
2. In class2.m, enter the code in **Listing 8.14**.
   This code creates the `Class2` class.
3. In class2.m, add the code to create the `print` method (**Listing 8.15**).
4. Save class2.m.
5. Create a header file named **class2.h**.
6. In class2.h, enter the code in **Listing 8.16**.
7. Save class2.h.

```
#import <stdio.h>
#include <Foundation/Foundation.h>
#import "Class1.h"
#import "Class2.h"

@implementation Class2
        .
        .
        .
@end
```

Listing 8.14 Starting class2.m.

```
#import <stdio.h>
#include <Foundation/Foundation.h>
#import "Class1.h"
#import "Class1.h"

@implementation Class2
-(void) print
{
   printf("This is Class 2.\n");
}
@end
```

Listing 8.15 The class1.m program.

```
#include <Foundation/Foundation.h>
#import "Class1.h"

@interface Class2: Class1
-(void) print;
@end
```

Listing 8.16 The class2.h file.

```
#import <stdio.h>
#import "Class1.h"
#import "Class2.h"

int main(void) {
    Class1 *c = [Class1 new];

    [c print];
        .
        .
        .
```

Listing 8.17 Starting main.m.

```
#import <stdio.h>
#import "Class1.h"
#import "Class2.h"

int main(void) {
    Class1 *c = [Class1 new];

    [c print];

    [Class2 poseAsClass: [Class1 class]];

    Class1 *c2 = [Class1 new];

    [c2 print];

    return 0;
}
```

Listing 8.18 The main.m program.

Posing: Putting It All Together

To make posing happen, you use the `poseAsClass` keyword. In the example here, to make `Class2` pose as `Class1`, you can use this line:

```
[Class2 poseAsClass: [Class1 class]];
```

From then on, when you create an object of `Class1`, you'll really be creating an object of `Class2`, as you'll see in this task.

To make one class pose as another:

1. Create a new program named **main.m**.
2. In main.m, enter the code shown in **Listing 8.17**.

   This code creates an object of `Class1` and calls its `print` method.
3. Add the code to make `Class2` pose as `Class1`, create an object of `Class1`, and call its `print` method (**Listing 8.18**).

   This time, it's actually the `Class2` `print` method that will be called.

continues on next page

4. Save main.m.
5. If you're using Linux, UNIX, or Windows, create a makefile named **GNUmakefile** as shown in **Listing 8.19**.
6. Run the main.m posing program.

   You should see:

   ```
   This is Class 1.
   This is Class 2.
   ```

```
include $(GNUSTEP_MAKEFILES)/common.make

TOOL_NAME = posing
posing_OBJC_FILES = Class1.m Class2.m
main.m

include $(GNUSTEP_MAKEFILES)/tool.make
```

Listing 8.19 GNUmakefile.

About Protocols

Protocols let you specify an interface for a method or methods that can be used in multiple classes. For instance, if you have a method named `print` and want to create a protocol for it, you can do that in a file named, say, printing.h:

```
@protocol Printing
-(void) print;
@end
```

Then you can include printing.h in the interface files of other classes. Doing so adds `print` to the interfaces of those classes in the header file for `Class1`:

```
#include <Foundation/Foundation.h>
#import "printing.h"

@interface Class1: NSObject
-(void) print;
@end
```

And you can also include printing.h in another class header, for `Class2`:

```
#include "Class1.h"
#import "printing.h"

@interface Class2: Class1
@end
```

Now you can implement `print` one way for `Class1`:

```
#import <stdio.h>
#include <Foundation/Foundation.h>
#import "Class1.h"

@implementation Class1
-(void) print
{
   printf("This is Class 1.\n");
}
@end
```

continues on next page

And you can implement print another way for Class2:

```
#import <stdio.h>
#include <Foundation/Foundation.h>
#import "Class1.h"
#import "Class2.h"

@implementation Class2
-(void) print
{
   printf("This is Class 2.\n");
}
@end
```

Then you can create objects of Class1 and Class1 and call each of their print methods like this:

```
#import <stdio.h>
#import "Class1.h"
#import "Class2.h"

int main(void) {
   Class1 *c = [Class1 new];
   [c print];

   Class2 *c2 = [Class2 new];
   [c2 print];

   return 0;
}
```

And each of these print methods will be different, so although there was only one protocol, there are two different implementations.

Protocols let you define the interface of a method in this way. Although Objective-C has no true multiple inheritance capability, you can use multiple protocols (not classes) as the basis for derived classes. The protocols say what methods you're including and specify their return types, but it's up to you to implement those methods in the derived classes. That's as close as Objective-C gets to multiple inheritance (in true multiple inheritance, you can derive a class from multiple base classes).

Protocols: Defining the Protocol and Interfaces

When you define a protocol for a method or methods, you usually store that protocol in a header file. You'll create a protocol named `Printing` for a method named `print` in a file named printing.h:

```
@protocol Printing
-(void) print;
@end
```

Then you'll use that protocol for one class in an interface file named ClassFirst.h:

```
#include <Foundation/Foundation.h>
#import "printing.h"

@interface Class1: NSObject
-(void) print;
@end
```

You'll also use the `Printing` protocol in an interface file, ClassSecond.h, for a class derived from that first class:

```
#include "Class1.h"
#import "printing.h"

@interface Class2: Class1
@end
```

Then you'll implement the `print` method for `Class1` and `Class2` in different ways (in the next task).

To define the protocol and interfaces:

1. Create a new file named **printing.h**.
2. In printing.h, enter the code shown in **Listing 8.20**.

   This code creates the protocol for the `print` method.
3. Save printing.h.
4. Create a new file named **ClassFirst.h**.
5. In ClassFirst.h, enter the code to create the interface for the first class, which makes use of the new protocol we've defined (**Listing 8.21**).
6. Save ClassFirst.h.
7. Create a new file named **ClassSecond.h**.
8. In ClassSecond.h, store the code to set up the interface for the second class, which is derived from the first class and also makes use of the new protocol for the `print` method (**Listing 8.22**).
9. Save ClassSecond.h.

```
@protocol Printing
-(void) print;
@end
```

Listing 8.20 The printing.h file.

```
#include <Foundation/Foundation.h>
#import "printing.h"

@interface Class1: NSObject
-(void) print;
@end
```

Listing 8.21 The ClassFirst.h file.

```
#include "Class1.h"
#import "printing.h"

@interface Class2: Class1
@end
```

Listing 8.22 The ClassSecond.h file.

```
#import <stdio.h>
#include <Foundation/Foundation.h>
#import "Class1.h"

@implementation Class1
        .
        .
        .
@end
```

Listing 8.23 Starting ClassFirst.m.

```
#import <stdio.h>
#include <Foundation/Foundation.h>
#import "Class1.h"

@implementation Class1
-(void) print
{
    printf("This is Class 1.\n");
}
@end
```

Listing 8.24 The ClassFirst.m program.

Protocols: Creating the Class Implementations

Now that you've defined the protocol and used it in the interfaces with two classes, you need to define the implementation of the method in the protocol, here named `print`.

To define the implementation with protocols:

1. Create a new program named **ClassFirst.m**.
2. In ClassFirst.m, enter the code shown in **Listing 8.23**.

   This code creates the implementation of `Class1`.
3. Add the code to create the implementation of the `print` method (**Listing 8.24**).
4. Save ClassFirst.m.
5. Create a new program named **ClassSecond.m**.

continues on next page

6. In ClassSecond.m, enter the code shown in **Listing 8.25**.

   This code creates the implementation of `Class2`.

7. In ClassSecond.m, add the code to create the implementation of the `print` method in `Class2` (**Listing 8.26**).

8. Save ClassSecond.m.

```
#import <stdio.h>
#include <Foundation/Foundation.h>
#import "Class1.h"
#import "Class2.h"

@implementation Class2
        .
        .
        .
@end
```

Listing 8.25 Starting ClassSecond.m.

```
#import <stdio.h>
#include <Foundation/Foundation.h>
#import "Class1.h"
#import "Class2.h"

@implementation Class2
-(void) print
{
   printf("This is Class 2.\n");
}
@end
```

Listing 8.26 The ClassSecond.m program.

```
#import <stdio.h>
#import "Class1.h"
#import "Class2.h"

int main(void) {
    Class1 *c = [Class1 new];
    [c print];
        .
        .
        .
    return 0;
}
```

Listing 8.27 Starting main.m.

```
#import <stdio.h>
#import "Class1.h"
#import "Class2.h"

int main(void) {
    Class1 *c = [Class1 new];
    [c print];

    Class2 *c2 = [Class2 new];
    [c2 print];

    return 0;
}
```

Listing 8.28 The main.m program.

Protocols: Putting It All Together

Now that you've defined a protocol for the `print` method and implemented that method in two classes, you can create objects of those classes and call the `print` method in each:

```
int main(void) {
    Class1 *c = [Class1 new];
    [c print];

    Class2 *c2 = [Class2 new];
    [c2 print];

    return 0;
}
```

Each method will print a different method, so although the protocol defines an interface for one method, the actual implementation depends on the classes that put the method to use.

To use protocols:

1. Create a new program named **main.m**.
2. In main.m, enter the code shown in **Listing 8.27**.

   This code creates an object of the first class and executes its `print` method.
3. Add the code to create an object of the second class and execute its `print` method as well (**Listing 8.28**).

continues on next page

4. Save main.m.

5. If you're using Linux, UNIX, or Windows, create a makefile named **GNUmakefile** as shown in **Listing 8.29**.

6. Run the main.m protocols program.

   You should see the following:

```
This is Class 1.
This is Class 2.
```

```
include $(GNUSTEP_MAKEFILES)/common.make

TOOL_NAME = protocols
protocols_OBJC_FILES = ClassFirst.m
ClassSecond.m main.m

include $(GNUSTEP_MAKEFILES)/tool.make
```

Listing 8.29 GNUmakefile.

Using Arrays and Dictionaries

9

In this chapter, we're going to explore two important features of the Objective-C Foundation classes: arrays and dictionaries.

You saw C-style arrays in Chapter 3. Those arrays let you handle your data as a set of values accessible by index. For example, here's how to create a standard array and display some information about it:

```
#include <stdio.h>

int main()
{
  int scores[5] = {92 , 73 , 57 , 98 ,
    89 };

  printf(
    "The array is %i elements long.",
    sizeof(scores) / sizeof(int));

  return 0;
}
```

In this chapter, you're going to build arrays using the Foundation classes that come with Objective-C. Those array classes let you do more with arrays, such as sort them, as you'll see in this chapter.

continues on next page

You can also create dictionaries in Objective-C using the Foundation classes. A dictionary in Objective-C is just like an array, but it uses words as index values, not numerical values. So while an array might be indexed by the numbers 0, 1, 2, 3, and so on, a dictionary would use the index terms "zero," "one," "two," "three," and so on. The index values need not be sequential; you could as well have used "banana," "apple," and "orange."

In addition, you can create mutable arrays and dictionaries: that is, arrays and dictionaries whose length can be changed on the fly in your code. You'll see how that works here.

All that and more is coming up in this chapter, which includes: the `NSArray`, `NSMutableArray`, `NSMutableDictionary`, and `NSDictionary` classes, as well as some others.

```
#import <Foundation/Foundation.h>

int main()
{
  NSArray *array = [[NSArray alloc]
  initWithObjects: @"red", @"white",
  @"blue", nil];
          .
          .
          .
  return 0;
}
```

Listing 9.1 Starting createarray.m.

```
#import <Foundation/Foundation.h>

int main()
{
  NSArray *array = [[NSArray alloc]
  initWithObjects: @"red", @"white",
  @"blue", nil];

  printf("Array has been created.");

  return 0;
}
```

Listing 9.2 The createarray.m program.

Creating an Array

You can create an array using the Foundation class `NSArray`. Such arrays are static and cannot be changed at run time..

Here's how you might create such an array, initializing it to `"red"`, `"white"`, and `"blue"`.

```
#import <Foundation/Foundation.h>

int main()
{
  NSArray *array = [[NSArray alloc]
  initWithObjects: @"red", @"white",
  @"blue", nil];
          .
          .
          .
}
```

To create a static array:

1. Create a program named **createarray.m**.
2. In createarray.m, enter the code shown in **Listing 9.1**.

   This code creates the array and initializes it with data.
3. Add the code to display a message indicating success (**Listing 9.2**).
4. Save createarray.m.
5. Run the createarray.m program (ignoring the warning about the unused array variable).

   You should see the following:

   ```
   Array has been created.
   ```

✔ Tips

- It's a good idea to end all arrays with the `nil` object, and as previously discussed, be sure to use the @ sign to differentiate Objective-C strings from C-style strings:
- You'll need a GNUmakefile file as detailed in previous chapters if you're using Linux, UNIX, or Windows.

Accessing Array Elements

You created an array in the previous task. Now how do you access individual elements in that array? For example, what if you want to access the element at `array[0]`?

To do that, you send the array an `objectAtIndex` message along with the index value you want to access:

```
#import <Foundation/Foundation.h>

int main()
{
  NSArray *array = [[NSArray alloc]
  initWithObjects: @"red", @"white",
  @"blue", nil];

  printf("array[0] = %s", [[array
  objectAtIndex: 0] cString]);
}
```

In this task, you'll see how to access individual elements with the `objectAtIndex` message.

To access individual elements:

1. Create a program named **accesselements.m**.
2. In accesselements.m, enter the code shown in **Listing 9.3**.

   This code creates the array and initializes it with data.
3. Add the code to access the elements of your choice with the `objectAtIndex` message and turn the Objective-C string into a C-style string before passing it to the `printf()` function (**Listing 9.4**).
4. Save accesselements.m.
5. Run the accesselements.m program.

   You should see the following:

   `array[0] = red.`

```
#import <Foundation/Foundation.h>

int main()
{
  NSArray *array = [[NSArray alloc]
  initWithObjects: @"red", @"white",
  @"blue", nil];
        .
        .
        .
  return 0;
}
```

Listing 9.3 Starting accesselements.m.

```
#import <Foundation/Foundation.h>

int main()
{
  NSArray *array = [[NSArray alloc]
  initWithObjects: @"red", @"white",
  @"blue", nil];

  printf("array[0] = %s", [[array
  objectAtIndex: 0] cString]);

  return 0;
}
```

Listing 9.4 The accesselements.m program.

✔ Tip

- To insert an object into an array, you use the `insertObjectAtIndex` message.

```
#import <Foundation/Foundation.h>
#import <stdio.h>

int main( int argc, const char *argv[] ) {
  NSAutoreleasePool *pool =
[[NSAutoreleasePool alloc] init];

  NSArray *array = [[NSArray alloc]
    initWithObjects:
    @"red", @"white", @"blue", nil];

  NSEnumerator *enumerator = [array
    objectEnumerator];
  id obj;
        .
        .
        .
}
```

Listing 9.5 Starting enumerator.m.

Using Enumeration to Loop over an Array

Objective-C provides an easy way to loop over an array: you can use a `NSEnumerator` object. Here's how to create an enumerator for an array:

```
NSArray *array = [[NSArray alloc]
  initWithObjects:
  @"red", @"white", @"blue", nil];

NSEnumerator *enumerator = [array
  objectEnumerator];
```

Then you can use the enumerator's `nextObject` message to get the next element as you iterate the array in a loop.

To use enumeration to loop over an array:

1. Create a new program named **enumerator.m**.
2. In enumerator.m, enter the code shown in **Listing 9.5**.

   This code creates the array, an enumerator for the array, and a placeholder variable for objects from the array.

continues on next page

3. In enumerator.m, enter the code shown in **Listing 9.6**.

   This code uses the `nextObject` message to get the next object from the enumerator in a `while` loop. We also create an `NSAutoreleasePool` object to keep track of memory use.

4. Save enumerator.m.

5. If you're using Linux, UNIX, or Windows, create a new makefile named **GNUmakefile**.

6. Run the enumerator.m program.

   You should see the following:

   ```
   red
   white
   blue
   ```

✔ Tip

- If you want to loop over an array with a `for` loop, you can send the array the message `count` to get the number of elements in the array.

```
#import <Foundation/Foundation.h>
#import <stdio.h>

int main( int argc, const char *argv[] ) {
  NSAutoreleasePool *pool =
[[NSAutoreleasePool alloc] init];

  NSArray *array = [[NSArray alloc]
    initWithObjects:
    @"red", @"white", @"blue", nil];

  NSEnumerator *enumerator = [array
    objectEnumerator];
  id obj;

  while ((obj = [enumerator nextObject]))
  {
    printf("%s\n", [[obj description]
      cString]);
  }

  [pool release];

  return 0;
}
```

Listing 9.6 Editing enumerator.m.

```
#import <Foundation/Foundation.h>
#import <stdio.h>

int main( int argc, const char *argv[] ) {
  NSAutoreleasePool *pool =
[[NSAutoreleasePool alloc] init];

  NSMutableArray *array =
    [[NSMutableArray
    alloc] initWithObjects:
    @"red", @"white", @"blue", nil];

  NSEnumerator *enumerator = [array
    objectEnumerator];
  id obj;
        .
        .
        .
}
```

Listing 9.7 Starting createmutablearray.m.

Creating a Mutable Array

The arrays you create with NSArray are fixed arrays—you cannot change their length at run time. However, the length of arrays you create with the NSMutableArray class can be changed when your program runs.

In the next task, you'll use NSMutableArray to add elements to a mutable array.

To create a mutable array:

1. Create a new program named **createmutablearray.m**.
2. In createmutablearray.m, enter the code shown in **Listing 9.7**.

   This code creates the mutable array.

continues on next page

3. In createmutablearray.m, enter the code shown in **Listing 9.8**.

   This code uses an enumerator and the `nextObject` message to get the next object from the enumerator in a `while` loop.

4. Save createmutablearray.m.

5. If you're using Linux, UNIX, or Windows, create a new makefile named **GNUmakefile**.

6. Run the createmutablearray.m program. You should see the following:

   ```
   red
   white
   blue
   ```

   In the next task, you'll add elements to this mutable array.

```
#import <Foundation/Foundation.h>
#import <stdio.h>

int main( int argc, const char *argv[] ) {
  NSAutoreleasePool *pool =
[[NSAutoreleasePool alloc] init];

  NSMutableArray *array =
    [[NSMutableArray
    alloc] initWithObjects:
    @"red", @"white", @"blue", nil];

  NSEnumerator *enumerator = [array
    objectEnumerator];
  id obj;

  while ((obj = [enumerator nextObject]))
  {
    printf("%s\n", [[obj description]
      cString]);
  }

  [pool release];

  return 0;
}
```

Listing 9.8 Editing createmutablearray.m.

```
#import <Foundation/Foundation.h>
#import <stdio.h>

int main( int argc, const char *argv[] ) {
  NSAutoreleasePool *pool =
    [[NSAutoreleasePool alloc] init];

  NSMutableArray *array =
    [[NSMutableArray alloc]
    initWithObjects: @"red", @"white",
    @"blue", nil];
        .
        .
        .
}
```

Listing 9.9 Starting addelements.m.

Adding Elements to a Mutable Array

It's easy to add new elements to a mutable array at run time: you just send the `addObject` message.

To add elements to a mutable array:

1. Create a file named **addelements.m**.
2. In addelements.m, enter the code shown in **Listing 9.9**.

   This code creates the mutable array you'll use and initializes it to `"red"`, `"white"`, and `"blue"`.

continues on next page

3. Enter the code to add the elements "orange", "green", and "azure" and then loop over the array to print a list of all the elements (**Listing 9.10**).
4. Save addelements.m.
5. Run the addelements.m program.

   You should see the following:

```
red
white
blue
orange
green
azure
```

```
#import <Foundation/Foundation.h>
#import <stdio.h>

int main( int argc, const char *argv[] ) {
  NSAutoreleasePool *pool =
    [[NSAutoreleasePool alloc] init];

  NSMutableArray *array =
    [[NSMutableArray alloc]
    initWithObjects: @"red", @"white",
    @"blue", nil];

  NSEnumerator *enumerator = [array
    objectEnumerator];
  id obj;

  [array addObject: @"orange"];
  [array addObject: @"green"];
  [array addObject: @"azure"];

  while ((obj = [enumerator nextObject])) {
    printf("%s\n", [[obj description]
      cString]);
  }

  [pool release];

  return 0;
}
```

Listing 9.10 The addelements.m program.

```
#import <Foundation/Foundation.h>
#import <stdio.h>

int main( int argc, const char *argv[] ) {
  NSAutoreleasePool *pool =
    [[NSAutoreleasePool alloc] init];

  NSMutableArray *array =
    [[NSMutableArray alloc]
    initWithObjects: @"red", @"white",
    @"blue", nil];

  NSEnumerator *enumerator = [array
    objectEnumerator];
  id obj;

  [array addObject: @"orange"];
  [array addObject: @"green"];
  [array addObject: @"azure"];

  while ((obj = [enumerator nextObject])) {
    printf("%s\n", [[obj description]
      cString]);
  }
        .
        .
        .
```

Listing 9.11 Starting sortarray.m.

Sorting an Array

You can sort an array by sending it a `sortUsingSelector` message. For example, here's how you perform a case-insensitive sort, using the `caseInsensitiveCompare` selector:

```
[array sortUsingSelector: @selector(
  caseInsensitiveCompare:)];
```

To sort an array:

1. Create a file named **sortarray.m**.
2. In sortarray.m, enter the code shown in **Listing 9.11**.

   This code creates the array and prints it.

continues on next page

3. Add the code to sort the array and then print it (**Listing 9.12**).
4. Save sortarray.m.
5. Run the sortarray.m program.

   You should see the unsorted array followed by this:

   ```
   Sorting the array.
   azure
   blue
   green
   orange
   red
   white
   ```

```
#import <Foundation/Foundation.h>
#import <stdio.h>

int main( int argc, const char *argv[] ) {
  NSAutoreleasePool *pool =
    [[NSAutoreleasePool alloc] init];

  NSMutableArray *array =
    [[NSMutableArray alloc]
    initWithObjects: @"red", @"white",
    @"blue", nil];

  NSEnumerator *enumerator = [array
    objectEnumerator];
  id obj;

  [array addObject: @"orange"];
  [array addObject: @"green"];
  [array addObject: @"azure"];

  while ((obj = [enumerator nextObject])) {
    printf("%s\n", [[obj description]
      cString]);
  }

  printf("Sorting the array.\n");
  [array sortUsingSelector: @selector(
    caseInsensitiveCompare: )];

  NSEnumerator *enumerator2 = [array
    objectEnumerator];

  while ((obj = [enumerator2
    nextObject])) {
    printf("%s\n", [[obj description]
    cString]);
  }

  [pool release];
  return 0;
}
```

Listing 9.12 The sortarray.m program.

```
#import <Foundation/Foundation.h>
#import <stdio.h>

int main( int argc, const char *argv[] ) {
  NSAutoreleasePool *pool =
  [[NSAutoreleasePool alloc] init];

  NSMutableArray *array =
  [[NSMutableArray alloc]
  initWithObjects:
  @"red", @"white", @"blue", nil];

  NSEnumerator *enumerator = [array
    objectEnumerator];
  id obj;

  [array addObject: @"orange"];
  [array addObject: @"green"];
  [array addObject: @"azure"];

  while ((obj = [enumerator nextObject])) {
    printf("%s\n", [[obj description]
      cString]);
  }

  printf("Sorting the array.\n");
  [array sortUsingSelector: @selector(
    caseInsensitiveCompare: )];

  NSEnumerator *enumerator2 = [array
    objectEnumerator];

  while ((obj = [enumerator2
    nextObject])) {
    printf("%s\n", [[obj description]
      cString]);
  }

  printf("Freeing memory.\n");
  [array release];
  [pool release];

  return 0;
}
```

Listing 9.13 The releasememory.m program.

Releasing Array Memory

The memory used by a large array can be considerable. You can release the memory used for an array by sending the array a `release` message.

To release array memory:

1. Copy the sortarray.m program to a program named **releasememory.m.**
2. In releasememory.m, add the code highlighted in **Listing 9.13.**
3. Save releasememory.m.
4. Run the releasememory.m program. You should see the following:

```
red
white
blue
orange
green
azure
Sorting the array.
azure
blue
green
orange
red
white
Freeing memory.
```

Creating a Dictionary

A dictionary lets you use words or other objects as keys and retrieve or store objects accessed by that key. In this task, you'll create a dictionary to see how it works.

To create a dictionary:

1. Create a file named **createdictionary.m**.
2. In createdictionary.m, enter the code shown in **Listing 9.14**.

   This code creates the dictionary and adds keys and values to it.

continues on next page

```
#import <Foundation/Foundation.h>
#import <stdio.h>

int main()
{
  NSAutoreleasePool *pool =
    [[NSAutoreleasePool alloc] init];
  NSDictionary *dictionary =
    [[NSDictionary alloc]
    initWithObjectsAndKeys:
      @"banana", @"fruit",
      @"onion", @"vegetable",
      @"turkey", @"meat",
      nil];
}
      .
      .
      .
```

Listing 9.14 Starting createdictionary.m.

```
#import <Foundation/Foundation.h>
#import <stdio.h>

int main()
{
  NSAutoreleasePool *pool =
    [[NSAutoreleasePool alloc] init];
  NSDictionary *dictionary =
    [[NSDictionary alloc]
    initWithObjectsAndKeys:
      @"banana", @"fruit",
      @"onion", @"vegetable",
      @"turkey", @"meat",
      nil];

  printf("Entry for fruit: %s\n",
 [[dictionary objectForKey:@"fruit"]
    cString]);

  [dictionary release];
  [pool release];

  return 0;
}
```

Listing 9.15 The createdictionary.m program.

3. Add the code to display the value for a particular key (**Listing 9.15**).
4. Save createdictionary.m.
5. Run the createdictionary.m program.

   You should see the unsorted array followed by this:

   `Entry for fruit: banana`

Enumerating a Dictionary

You can use an enumerator object to loop over a dictionary just as you can use an enumerator to loop over an array. In this task, you'll use an enumerator to print the keys and values of an dictionary.

To enumerate a dictionary:

1. Create a new program named **enumeratordictionary.m**.
2. In enumeratordictionary.m, enter the code shown in **Listing 9.16**.

   This code creates the dictionary you'll use.

```
#import <Foundation/Foundation.h>
#import <stdio.h>

int main()
{
  NSAutoreleasePool *pool =
    [[NSAutoreleasePool alloc] init];
  NSDictionary *dictionary =
    [[NSDictionary alloc]
   initWithObjectsAndKeys:
    @"banana", @"fruit",
    @"onion", @"vegetable",
    @"turkey", @"meat",
    nil];
        .
        .
        .
```

Listing 9.16 Starting enumeratordictionary.m.

```
#import <Foundation/Foundation.h>
#import <stdio.h>

int main()
{
  NSAutoreleasePool *pool =
    [[NSAutoreleasePool alloc] init];
  NSDictionary *dictionary =
    [[NSDictionary alloc]
   initWithObjectsAndKeys:
    @"banana", @"fruit",
    @"onion", @"vegetable",
    @"turkey", @"meat",
    nil];

  NSEnumerator *enumerator = [dictionary
    keyEnumerator];
  id key;

  while ((key = [enumerator nextObject]))
  {
    printf( "%s => %s\n",
     [[key description] cString],
     [[[dictionary objectForKey: key]
       description] cString] );
  }

  [dictionary release];
  [pool release];

  return 0;
}
```

Listing 9.17 The enumeratordictionary.m program.

3. Add the code to create the enumerator and loop over the dictionary (**Listing 9.17**).
4. Save enumeratordictionary.m.
5. Run the enumeratordictionary.m program.
   You should see the following:
   ```
   vegetable => onion
   meat => turkey
   fruit => banana
   ```

Creating a Mutable Dictionary

You can extend a mutable dictionary by adding new items or reduce it by removing items. You'll see how to create a mutable dictionary in this task, and you'll see how to extend it in code in the next task.

To create a mutable dictionary:

1. Create a new program named **createmutabledictionary.m.**
2. In createmutabledictionary.m, enter the code shown in **Listing 9.18**.

   This code creates an object of the `NSMutableDictionary` class.
3. Add the code to display a message indicating that the creation process went smoothly and to deallocate the memory used by the mutable dictionary before ending the program (**Listing 9.19**).
4. Save createmutabledictionary.m.
5. Run the createmutabledictionary.m program.

   You should see the following:

   `Created mutable dictionary.`

```
#import <Foundation/Foundation.h>
#import <stdio.h>

int main()
{
  NSAutoreleasePool *pool =
    [[NSAutoreleasePool alloc] init];
  NSMutableDictionary *dictionary =
    [[NSMutableDictionary alloc] init];
        .
        .
        .
```

Listing 9.18 Starting createmutabledictionary.m.

```
#import <Foundation/Foundation.h>
#import <stdio.h>

int main()
{
  NSAutoreleasePool *pool =
    [[NSAutoreleasePool alloc] init];
  NSMutableDictionary *dictionary =
    [[NSMutableDictionary alloc] init];

  printf(
    "Created mutable dictionary.\n");

  [dictionary release];
  [pool release];

  return 0;
}
```

Listing 9.19 The createmutabledictionary.m program.

```
#import <Foundation/Foundation.h>
#import <stdio.h>

int main()
{
  NSAutoreleasePool *pool =
    [[NSAutoreleasePool alloc] init];
  NSMutableDictionary *dictionary =
    [[NSMutableDictionary alloc] init];

  [dictionary setObject: @"banana"
    forKey: @"fruit"];
  [dictionary setObject: @"onion" forKey:
    @"vegetable" ];
  [dictionary setObject: @"turkey"
    forKey: @"meat" ];
        .
        .
        .
```

Listing 9.20 Starting addkeys.m.

Adding Objects to a Mutable Dictionary

In the previous task, you created a mutable dictionary, but didn't add any data to it. In this task, you'll add keys and values to the mutable dictionary.

To add objects to a mutable dictionary:

1. Create a new program named **addkeys.m**.
2. In addkeys.m, enter the code shown in **Listing 9.20**.

   This code creates the mutable dictionary and uses the `addObject` message to add key and value pairs to the dictionary.

continues on next page

3. Add the code to print the contents of the mutable dictionary (**Listing 9.21**).
4. Save addkeys.m.
5. Run the protected addkeys.m program. You should see the following:

```
vegetable => onion
meat => turkey
fruit => banana
```

```
#import <Foundation/Foundation.h>
#import <stdio.h>

int main()
{
  NSAutoreleasePool *pool =
    [[NSAutoreleasePool alloc] init];
  NSMutableDictionary *dictionary =
    [[NSMutableDictionary alloc] init];

  [dictionary setObject: @"banana"
    forKey: @"fruit"];
  [dictionary setObject: @"onion" forKey:
    @"vegetable" ];
  [dictionary setObject: @"turkey"
    forKey: @"meat" ];

  NSEnumerator *enumerator = [dictionary
    keyEnumerator];
  id key;

  while ((key = [enumerator nextObject]))
  {
    printf( "%s => %s\n",
     [[key description] cString],
     [[[dictionary objectForKey: key]
       description] cString] );
  }

  [dictionary release];
  [pool release];

  return 0;
}
```

Listing 9.21 The addkeys.m program.

Managing Memory in Objective-C

In this chapter, you'll learn about memory management in Objective-C. Objective-C keeps track of all the objects you create with a retain count, and when that count goes down to zero, Objective-C automatically deallocates the memory allocated to an object.

For example, say that you create two objects:

```
Class1 *object1 = [[Class1 alloc]
  init];
Class1 *object2 = [[Class1 alloc]
  init];
```

Now the retain count of each object is 1, as you can verify by asking each object what its retain count is and printing that result:

```
printf("object1  retain count: %i\n",
  [object1 retainCount]);
printf("object2 retain count: %i\n",
  [object2 retainCount]);
```

You can also explicitly increment the retain count yourself, like this:.

```
[object1 retain];
[object1 retain];
[object2 retain];
```

continues on next page

When you pass an object the `retain` message, it increments its own retain count. So in this case, the retain count for `object1` would increase from 1 to 2 to 3, and the retain count for `object2` would increase from 1 to 2.

To decrement the retain count, you send an object a `release` message:

```
[object1 release];
[object2 release];
```

These two lines of code reduce the retain count of `object1` to 2 and the retain count of `object2` to 1.

When you send a `release` message that reduces the retain count of an object to 0, Objective-C automatically deallocates that object. You'll implement the `dealloc` method for objects yourself in this chapter to see how Objective-C deallocates your objects.

```
#import <Foundation/Foundation.h>
#import <stdio.h>

@interface Class1: NSObject
@end

@implementation Class1
@end

int main(void)
{
  Class1 *object1 = [[Class1 alloc]
    init];
  Class1 *object2 = [[Class1 alloc]
    init];
        .
        .
        .
```

Listing 10.1 Starting createobject.m.

```
#import <Foundation/Foundation.h>
#import <stdio.h>

@interface Class1: NSObject
@end

@implementation Class1
@end

int main(void)
{
  Class1 *object1 = [[Class1 alloc]
    init];
  Class1 *object2 = [[Class1 alloc]
    init];

  printf("Created object1\n");
  printf("Created object2\n");

  return 0;
}
```

Listing 10.2 The createobject.m program.

Creating Test Objects

In this task, you'll create two test objects whose retain count you'll track in the upcoming tasks as you increase and decrease the retain count.

The two objects will be objects of `Class1`, which just looks like this (you'll add methods to this class in a later task):

```
@interface Class1: NSObject
@end

@implementation Class1
@end
```

All right—now let's create the test objects.

To create test objects:

1. Create a program named **createobject.m**.
2. In createobject.m, enter the code shown in **Listing 10.1**.
   This code creates the two test objects.
3. Add the code to display a message indicating success (**Listing 10.2**).
4. Save createobject.m.
5. Run the createobject.m program (ignoring the warning about not using the objects).
   You should see the following:
   ```
   Created object1
   Created object2
   ```

Displaying the Retain Count

When you create objects, Objective-C keeps track of them with a retain count. To find out what that retain count is, you send an object a `retainCount` message.

For example, in the previous task, you created two new objects:

```
Class1 *object1 = [[Class1 alloc]
  init];
Class1 *object2 = [[Class1 alloc]
  init];
```

You can display their retain count (which will be 1) like this:

```
printf("object1 retain count: %i\n",
  [object1 retainCount]);
printf("object2 retain count: %i\n",
  [object2 retainCount]);
```

To display the retain count:

1. Create a program named **retaincount.m**.
2. In retaincount.m, enter the code shown in **Listing 10.3**.

   This code creates the two test objects.

```
#import <Foundation/Foundation.h>
#import <stdio.h>

@interface Class1: NSObject
@end

@implementation Class1
@end

int main(void)
{
  Class1 *object1 = [[Class1 alloc]
    init];
  Class1 *object2 = [[Class1 alloc]
    init];
      .
      .
      .
```

Listing 10.3 Starting retaincount.m.

```
#import <Foundation/Foundation.h>
#import <stdio.h>

@interface Class1: NSObject
@end

@implementation Class1
@end

int main(void)
{
  Class1 *object1 = [[Class1 alloc]
    init];
  Class1 *object2 = [[Class1 alloc]
    init];

  printf("object1 retain count: %i\n",
    [object1 retainCount]);
  printf("object2 retain count: %i\n",
    [object2 retainCount]);

  return 0;
}
```

Listing 10.4 The retaincount.m program.

3. Add the code to display the retain count of each new object (**Listing 10.4**).
4. Save retaincount.m.
5. Run the retaincount.m program.
   You should see the following:
   ```
   object1 retain count: 1
   object2 retain count: 1
   ```

Incrementing an Object's Retain Count

You can increment the retain count of an object yourself by sending it a `retain` message. In this task, you'll increment the retain counts of two objects and then verify that the retain counts were indeed incremented.

To increment the retain count:

1. Create a new program named **incrementcount.m**.
2. In incrementcount.m, enter the code shown in **Listing 10.5**.

   This code creates the two test objects and displays their retain counts.

```
#import <Foundation/Foundation.h>
#import <stdio.h>

@interface Class1: NSObject
@end

@implementation Class1
@end

int main(void)
{
  Class1 *object1 = [[Class1 alloc]
    init];
  Class1 *object2 = [[Class1 alloc]
    init];

  printf("object1 retain count: %i\n",
    [object1 retainCount]);
  printf("object2 retain count: %i\n",
    [object2 retainCount]);
        .
        .
        .
}
```

Listing 10.5 Starting incrementcount.m.

```
#import <Foundation/Foundation.h>
#import <stdio.h>

@interface Class1: NSObject
@end

@implementation Class1
@end

int main(void)
{
  Class1 *object1 = [[Class1 alloc]
    init];
  Class1 *object2 = [[Class1 alloc]
    init];

  printf("object1 retain count: %i\n",
    [object1 retainCount]);
  printf("object2 retain count: %i\n",
    [object2 retainCount]);

  [object1 retain];
  [object1 retain];
  [object2 retain];

  printf("object1 retain count: %i\n",
    [object1 retainCount]);
  printf("object2 retain count: %i\n",
    [object2 retainCount]);

  return 0;
}
```

Listing 10.6 The incrementcount.m program.

3. Add the code to increment the retain counts and display the results (**Listing 10.6**).
4. Save incrementcount.m.
5. Run the incrementcount.m program. You should see the following:

```
object1 retain count: 1
object2 retain count: 1
object1 retain count: 3
object2 retain count: 2
```

Decrementing an Object's Retain Count

You can decrement an object's retain count by sending it a `release` message. You do that here and confirm that the retain count has been decremented.

To decrement the retain count:

1. Create a new program named **decrementcount.m**.
2. In decrementcount.m, enter the code shown in **Listing 10.7**.

   This code creates the two test objects and increments their retain counts.

```
#import <Foundation/Foundation.h>
#import <stdio.h>

@interface Class1: NSObject
@end

@implementation Class1
@end

int main(void)
{
  Class1 *object1 = [[Class1 alloc]
    init];
  Class1 *object2 = [[Class1 alloc]
    init];

  printf("object1 retain count: %i\n",
    [object1 retainCount]);
  printf("object2 retain count: %i\n",
    [object2 retainCount]);

  [object1 retain];
  [object1 retain];
  [object2 retain];

  printf("object1 retain count: %i\n",
    [object1 retainCount]);
  printf("object2 retain count: %i\n",
    [object2 retainCount]);
        .
        .
        .
```

Listing 10.7 Starting decrementcount.m.

```
#import <Foundation/Foundation.h>
#import <stdio.h>

@interface Class1: NSObject
@end

@implementation Class1
@end

int main(void)
{
  Class1 *object1 = [[Class1 alloc]
    init];
  Class1 *object2 = [[Class1 alloc]
    init];

  printf("object1 retain count: %i\n",
    [object1 retainCount]);
  printf("object2 retain count: %i\n",
    [object2 retainCount]);

  [object1 retain];
  [object1 retain];
  [object2 retain];

  printf("object1 retain count: %i\n",
    [object1 retainCount]);
  printf("object2 retain count: %i\n",
    [object2 retainCount]);

  [object1 release];
  [object2 release];

  printf("object1 retain count: %i\n",
    [object1 retainCount]);
  printf("object2 retain count: %i\n",
    [object2 retainCount]);

  return 0;
}
```

Listing 10.8 Editing decrementcount.m.

3. Add the code to decrement the retain count of each object by 1 and display the resulting retain count for each object (**Listing 10.8**).
4. Save decrementcount.m.
5. Run the decrementcount.m program. You should see the following:

```
object1 retain count: 1
object2 retain count: 1
object1 retain count: 3
object2 retain count: 2
object1 retain count: 2
object2 retain count: 1
```

Deallocating Objects from Memory

When the retain count of an object reaches zero, Objective-C deallocates that object from memory. You'll see how this works by overriding your objects' `dealloc` method and displaying a message when the objects are deallocated.

To deallocate an object:

1. Create a new program named **dealloc.m**.
2. In dealloc.m, enter the code shown in **Listing 10.9**.

   This code overrides the `Class1` `dealloc` method to display a message confirming the deallocation.

```
#import <Foundation/Foundation.h>
#import <stdio.h>

@interface Class1: NSObject
-(void) dealloc;
@end

@implementation Class1
-(void) dealloc
{
  printf("Deallocing the object\n");
  [super dealloc];
}
@end
        .
        .
        .
```

Listing 10.9 Starting dealloc.m.

```
#import <Foundation/Foundation.h>
#import <stdio.h>

@interface Class1: NSObject
-(void) dealloc;
@end

@implementation Class1
-(void) dealloc
{
  printf("Deallocing the object\n");
  [super dealloc];
}
@end

int main(void)
{
  Class1 *object1 = [[Class1 alloc]
    init];
  Class1 *object2 = [[Class1 alloc]
    init];

  printf("object1 retain count: %i\n",
    [object1 retainCount]);
  printf("object2 retain count: %i\n",
    [object2 retainCount]);

  [object1 retain];
  [object1 retain];
  [object2 retain];

  printf("object1 retain count: %i\n",
    [object1 retainCount]);
  printf("object2 retain count: %i\n",
    [object2 retainCount]);

  [object1 release];
  [object2 release];

  printf("object1 retain count: %i\n",
    [object1 retainCount]);
  printf("object2 retain count: %i\n",
    [object2 retainCount]);

  [object1 release];
  [object1 release];
  [object2 release];

  return 0;
}
```

Listing 10.10 Editing dealloc.m.

3. Add the code shown in **Listing 10.10**.

   This code creates two `Class1` objects and increments and decrements the retain counts of `object1` and `object2`, finally setting their retain counts to zero. At that point, Objective-C deallocates the objects, as confirmed by a message from the overridden `dealloc` method.

4. Save dealloc.m.

5. Run the dealloc.m program.

   You should see the following:

```
object1 retain count: 1
object2 retain count: 1
object1 retain count: 3
object2 retain count: 2
object1 retain count: 2
object2 retain count: 1
Deallocing the object
Deallocing the object
```

Using an Autorelease Pool

If you use `alloc` or `new` to create an object, you're responsible for managing the object's memory yourself (if memory is a concern). But for objects that you don't create with `alloc` or `new`, you can have Objective-C manage them for you using an autorelease pool.

Just create a `pool` object, and the objects will be placed in it automatically. At the end of the program, you have only to release the pool to release all the objects.

To use an autorelease pool:

1. Create a file named **pool.m**.
2. In pool.m, enter the code shown in **Listing 10.11**.

   This code creates the pool and a pool-managed object: `string1`.
3. Add the code to print the object's retain count and release the pool when the program ends (**Listing 10.12**).
4. Save pool.m.
5. Run the pool.m program.

   You should see the following:

   `Pool-managed string's retain count: 1`

```
#import <Foundation/Foundation.h>
#import <stdio.h>

int main()
{
  NSAutoreleasePool *pool =
    [[NSAutoreleasePool alloc] init];
  NSString *string1 = [NSString
    stringWithString: @"Pool-managed
    string"];
        .
        .
        .
}
```

Listing 10.11 Starting pool.m.

```
#import <Foundation/Foundation.h>
#import <stdio.h>

int main()
{
  NSAutoreleasePool *pool =
    [[NSAutoreleasePool alloc] init];
  NSString *string1 = [NSString
    stringWithString: @"Pool-managed
    string"];

  printf("%s's retain count: %x\n",
  [string1 cString], [string1
  retainCount] );

  [pool release];

  return 0;
}
```

Listing 10.12 The pool.m program.

```
#import <Foundation/Foundation.h>
#import <stdio.h>

int main()
{
  NSAutoreleasePool *pool =
  [[NSAutoreleasePool alloc] init];
  NSString *string1 = [NSString
  stringWithString: @"Pool-managed
  string"];
  NSString *string2 = [[NSString alloc]
  initWithString: @"Self-managed
  string"];

  printf("%s's retain count: %x\n",
  [string1 cString], [string1
  retainCount] );
        .
        .
        .
```

Listing 10.13 Editing pool.m.

Using Self-Managed Memory

If you create objects using `alloc` or `new`, you're responsible for managing their memory yourself (if memory is a concern). That means that when you're done with an object and want to release its memory, it's up to you to do so until its retain count reaches zero and Objective-C deallocates it.

In this task, you'll add a self-managed object to the previous task's pool.m program so you can compare the procedures for self-managed memory and pool-managed memory.

To use self-managed memory for an object:

1. Open pool.m.
2. Add the code to create a self-managed string (**Listing 10.13**).

continues on next page

3. Add the code to print the self-managed string's retain count and release the object (**Listing 10.14**).
4. Save pool.m.
5. Run the edited pool.m program.
   You should see the following:
   ```
   Pool-managed string's retain count: 1
   Self-managed string's retain count: 1
   ```

```
#import <Foundation/Foundation.h>
#import <stdio.h>

int main()
{
  NSAutoreleasePool *pool =
  [[NSAutoreleasePool alloc] init];
  NSString *string1 = [NSString
  stringWithString: @"Pool-managed
  string"];
  NSString *string2 = [[NSString alloc]
  initWithString: @"Self-managed
  string"];

  printf("%s's retain count: %x\n",
  [string1 cString], [string1
  retainCount] );

  printf("%s's retain count: %x\n",
  [string2 cString], [string2
  retainCount] );

  [string2 release];

  [pool release];

  return 0;
}
```

Listing 10.14 The edited pool.m program.

```
#import <Foundation/Foundation.h>
#import <stdio.h>

@interface Friend: NSObject
{
  NSString *firstName;
  NSString *lastName;
}
-(Friend*) initWithName: (NSString*)
  first lastName: (NSString*) last;
-(void) setName: (NSString*) first
  lastName: (NSString*) last;
-(void) print;
@end

@implementation Friend
-(Friend*) initWithName: (NSString*)
  first lastName: (NSString*) last
{
  self = [super init];

  if (self) {
    [self setName: first lastName: last];
  }

  return self;
}

-(void) setName: (NSString*) first
  lastName: (NSString*) last
{
  [self setFirst: first];
  [self setLast: last];
}

-(void) print
{
  printf("Your friend's name is %s %s",
    [firstName cString], [lastName
    cString]);
}
@end
```

Listing 10.15 Creating friends.m.

Deallocating Memory Yourself: Creating the Class

If you create objects of your own classes that store other objects internally, you're responsible for releasing the internal objects when the overall object is deallocated.

In the remaining tasks in this chapter, you'll see how this works using an example class named `Friend` that internally stores two `NSString` objects that correspond to the friend's first and last names. When the `Friend` object is deallocated, you'll manually release the two internal strings.

To create the Friend class:

1. Create a file named **friends.m**.
2. In friends.m, enter the code shown in **Listing 10.15**.

   This code creates the `Friend` class and internally stores the friend's first and last names.
3. Save friends.m.

Deallocating Memory Yourself: Storing Internal Objects

In this task, you'll continue working with the `Friend` class from the previous task. Here, you'll internally store the friend's first and last names as `NSString` objects.

To store internal objects:

1. Open friends.m.

```
#import <Foundation/Foundation.h>
#import <stdio.h>

@interface Friend: NSObject
{
  NSString *firstName;
  NSString *lastName;
}
-(Friend*) initWithName: (NSString*)
  first lastName: (NSString*) last;
-(void) setName: (NSString*) first
  lastName: (NSString*) last;
-(void) setFirst: (NSString*) first;
-(void) setLast: (NSString*) last;
-(void) print;
@end

@implementation Friend
-(Friend*) initWithName: (NSString*)
  first lastName: (NSString*) last
{
  self = [super init];

  if (self) {
    [self setName: first lastName: last];
  }

  return self;
}

-(void) setName: (NSString*) first
  lastName: (NSString*) last
{
  [self setFirst: first];
  [self setLast: last];
}
```

(code continues on next page)

Listing 10.16 Editing friends.m.

```
-(void) setFirst: (NSString*) first
{
  [first retain];
  [firstName release];
  firstName = first;
}

-(void) setLast: (NSString*) last
{
  [last retain];
  [lastName release];
  lastName = last;
}

-(void) print
{
  printf("Your friend's name is %s %s",
    [firstName cString], [lastName
    cString]);
}
@end
```

Listing 10.16 *continued*

2. Add the code to store the friend's first and last names in the `Friend` object as `NSString` objects (**Listing 10.16**).

3. Save friends.m.

Deallocating Memory Yourself: Creating the main Method

In this task, you'll create the `main` method for the deallocation example to release any internal objects when the containing object is deallocated.

To create the main method:

1. Open friends.m.
2. Add the code to create an object of the `Friend` class named `dan` (**Listing 10.17**).
3. Add the code to print the friend's name and release the `Friend` object (**Listing 10.18**).
4. Save friends.m.

```
int main(void)
{
  NSString *first =[[NSString alloc]
    initWithCString: "Dan"];
  NSString *last = [[NSString alloc]
    initWithCString: "Green"];

  Friend *dan = [[Friend alloc]
    initWithName: first lastName: last];

  [first release];
  [last release];
        .
        .
        .

}
```

Listing 10.17 Editing friends.m.

```
int main(void)
{
  NSString *first =[[NSString alloc]
    initWithCString: "Dan"];
  NSString *last = [[NSString alloc]
    initWithCString: "Green"];

  Friend *dan = [[Friend alloc]
    initWithName: first lastName: last];

  [first release];
  [last release];

  [dan print];

  [dan release];

  return 0;
}
```

Listing 10.18 Editing friends.m.

Deallocating Memory Yourself: Performing Deallocation

This task completes the examples illustrating how to release internal memory for custom objects. Here, you actually release the internally stored objects when the whole object is deallocated.

To deallocate internal memory:

1. Open friends.m.
2. Add the code to release the internal strings when the complete `Friend` object is deallocated (**Listing 10.19**).

continues on next page

```
#import <Foundation/Foundation.h>
#import <stdio.h>

@interface Friend: NSObject
{
  NSString *firstName;
  NSString *lastName;
}
-(Friend*) initWithName: (NSString*)
  first lastName: (NSString*) last;
-(void) setName: (NSString*) first
  lastName: (NSString*) last;
-(void) setFirst: (NSString*) first;
-(void) setLast: (NSString*) last;
-(void) print;
@end

@implementation Friend
-(Friend*) initWithName: (NSString*)
  first lastName: (NSString*) last
{
  self = [super init];

  if (self) {
    [self setName: first lastName: last];
  }

  return self;
}

-(void) setName: (NSString*) first
  lastName: (NSString*) last
{
  [self setFirst: first];
  [self setLast: last];
}

-(void) setFirst: (NSString*) first
{
  [first retain];
  [firstName release];
  firstName = first;
}
```

(code continues on next page)

Listing 10.19 Editing friends.m.

3. Save friends.m.

4. Run the friends.m program.

   You should see the following:

   `Your friend's name is Dan Green`

   The `Friends` object is deallocated, and its internally stored objects, `first` and `last`, are released.

```
-(void) setLast: (NSString*) last
{
  [last retain];
  [lastName release];
  lastName = last;
}

-(void) print
{
  printf("Your friend's name is %s %s",
    [firstName cString], [lastName
    cString]);
}

-(void) dealloc
{
  [firstName release];
  [lastName release];
  [super dealloc];
}
@end

int main(void)
{
  NSString *first =[[NSString alloc]
    initWithCString: "Dan"];
  NSString *last = [[NSString alloc]
    initWithCString: "Green"];

  Friend *dan = [[Friend alloc]
    initWithName: first lastName: last];

  [first release];
  [last release];

  [dan print];

  [dan release];

  return 0;
}
```

Listing 10.19 *continued*

11 Exception Handling

Errors are a fact of life. Even the most perfect programmer has code that creates run-time errors at times. This chapter is about handling such cases.

You'll commonly encounter two kinds of errors: compile-time errors and run-time errors. Compile-time errors are those raised by the compiler, and you have to fix those before you continue with your program. Run-time errors happen at run-time, even though your code compiled fine. Run-time errors are commonly called exceptions.

Objective-C can handle exceptions, but the way it does so varies by platform. In this chapter, we'll use the GNUstep way of handling exceptions, which is the most common method.

Here, you use macros like `NS_DURING` and `NS_HANDLER` to handle exceptions when they happen. For example, this code creates a custom exception and then reports on it:

```
#import <Foundation/Foundation.h>
#import <stdio.h>

int main()
{
  NSAutoreleasePool *pool =
    [[NSAutoreleasePool alloc] init];
```

continues on next page

```
NS_DURING
{
  NSException *myException =
    [[NSException
    alloc] initWithName: @"MyException"
     reason: @"Meltdown!" userInfo:
nil];

  [myException raise];

  [pool release];
}

NS_HANDLER
{
  printf("In error handler.\n");

  if ([[localException name]
    isEqualToString: @"MyException"])
  {
    printf("Meltdown error.\n");
  }

}

NS_ENDHANDLER
{
   printf("In end handler.");
}
return 0;
}
```

We'll take a look at the details in this chapter.

```
#import <Foundation/Foundation.h>
#import <stdio.h>

int main()
{
NS_DURING
{
        .
        .
        .
}

return 0;
}
```

Listing 11.1 Starting main.m.

```
#import <Foundation/Foundation.h>
#import <stdio.h>

int main()
{
NS_DURING
{
[Sensitive code]
}

return 0;
}
```

Listing 11.2 The main.m program.

Catching Exceptions

Whenever your code may cause an exception—for example, by dividing by zero—you can enclose it in a `NS_DURING` macro like this:

```
NS_DURING
{
[Sensitive code]
}
```

This is the first step in GNUstep exception handling: any exceptions that happen inside an `NS_DURING` macro can be handled in an `NS_HANDLER` macro, which is covered in the next task.

To catch exceptions:

1. Create a program named **main.m**.
2. In main.m, enter the code shown in **Listing 11.1**.

   This code creates an `NS_DURING` block.
3. Add your exception-prone code to the `NS_DURING` block (**Listing 11.2**).
4. Save main.m.

Handling Exceptions

When an exception occurs, you can handle that exception in an NS_HANDLER macro—that's where you place your exception-handling code, as you'll see in this task.

To handle exceptions:

1. Create a program named **main.m**.
2. In main.m, enter the code shown in **Listing 11.3**.

   This code creates the NS_DURING macro.
3. Enter the code to add the NS_HANDLER macro, which runs when an exception occurs (**Listing 11.4**).
4. Save main.m.

```
#import <Foundation/Foundation.h>
#import <stdio.h>

int main()
{

NS_DURING
{
        .
        .
        .
}



return 0;
}
```

Listing 11.3 Starting main.m.

```
#import <Foundation/Foundation.h>
#import <stdio.h>

int main()
{

NS_DURING
{
        .
        .
        .
}

NS_HANDLER
{
        .
        .
        .
}

return 0;
}
```

Listing 11.4 The main.m program.

```
#import <Foundation/Foundation.h>
#import <stdio.h>

int main()
{
NS_DURING
{
        .
        .
        .
}

NS_HANDLER
{
        .
        .
        .
}

return 0;
}
```

Listing 11.5 Starting main.m.

Using the End Handler

You can handle exceptions in the NS_HANDLER block. After the code in the NS_HANDLER block runs, you can have the code in another block, the NS_ENDHANDLER block, run, giving you a chance to add cleanup code.

To use the end handler:

1. Create a new program named **main.m**.
2. In main.m, enter the code shown in **Listing 11.5**.

   This code creates the NS_DURING and NS_HANDLER blocks.

continues on next page

3. Enter the code to add the NS_ENDHANDLER block for code you want executed after the NS_HANDLER block (**Listing 11.6**).
4. Save main.m.

```
#import <Foundation/Foundation.h>
#import <stdio.h>

int main()
{
NS_DURING
{
        .
        .
        .
}

NS_HANDLER
{
        .
        .
        .
}

NS_ENDHANDLER
{
        .
        .
        .
}
return 0;
}
```

Listing 11.6 The main.m program.

```
#import <Foundation/Foundation.h>
#import <stdio.h>

int main()
{
  NSAutoreleasePool *pool =
    [[NSAutoreleasePool alloc] init];

NS_DURING
{
  NSException *myException =
    [[NSException
    alloc] initWithName: @"MyException"
     reason: @"Meltdown!" userInfo: nil];

  [myException raise];

  [pool release];
}

NS_HANDLER
{
        .
        .
        .

}

NS_ENDHANDLER
{
        .
        .
        .
}
return 0;
}
```

Listing 11.7 Starting main.m.

Creating an Exception

Now you'll cause an exception to occur so you can handle it and confirm that your code works as expected.

In this task, you'll create an exception object; then you'll raise that exception, which causes the exception to actually occur. After that, you can catch and handle the exception.

To create an exception:

1. Create a new program named **main.m**.
2. In main.m, enter the code shown in **Listing 11.7**.

   This code creates an exception object and raises the exception.

continues on next page

3. Add the code to display a message from the exception handler and the exception end handler (**Listing 11.8**).
4. Save main.m.
5. Run the main.m program.

   You should see the following:

   ```
   In error handler.
   In end handler.
   ```

```
#import <Foundation/Foundation.h>
#import <stdio.h>

int main()
{
  NSAutoreleasePool *pool =
    [[NSAutoreleasePool alloc] init];

NS_DURING
{
  NSException *myException =
    [[NSException
    alloc] initWithName: @"MyException"
     reason: @"Meltdown!" userInfo: nil];

  [myException raise];

  [pool release];
}

NS_HANDLER
{
  printf("In error handler.\n");
}

NS_ENDHANDLER
{
   printf("In end handler.");
}
return 0;
}
```

Listing 11.8 The main.m program.

```
#import <Foundation/Foundation.h>
#import <stdio.h>

int main()
{
  NSAutoreleasePool *pool =
    [[NSAutoreleasePool alloc] init];

NS_DURING
{
  NSException *myException =
    [[NSException
    alloc] initWithName: @"MyException"
     reason: @"Meltdown!" userInfo: nil];

  [myException raise];

  [pool release];
}

NS_HANDLER
{
  printf("In error handler.\n");

}

NS_ENDHANDLER
{
   printf("In end handler.");
}
return 0;
}
```

Listing 11.9 Starting main.m.

Checking What Exception Occurred

In exception-handling blocks, you can refer to the exception that occurred as `localException`, an object built into Objective-C. Then you can find its name by sending it the `name` message—and so determine what exception occurred.

In this task, you'll determine what exception occurred and display a message to match.

To determine what exception occurred:

1. Create a new program named **main.m**.
2. In main.m, enter the code shown in **Listing 11.9**.

   This entry creates the exception and the exception-handling code.

continues on next page

3. Enter the code to check the name of the exception and display it (**Listing 11.10**).
4. Save main.m.
5. Run the main.m program.

   You should see the following:

   ```
   In error handler.
   Meltdown error.
   In end handler.
   ```

```
#import <Foundation/Foundation.h>
#import <stdio.h>

int main()
{
  NSAutoreleasePool *pool =
    [[NSAutoreleasePool alloc] init];

NS_DURING
{
  NSException *myException =
    [[NSException
    alloc] initWithName: @"MyException"
     reason: @"Meltdown!" userInfo: nil];

  [myException raise];

  [pool release];
}

NS_HANDLER
{
  printf("In error handler.\n");

  if ([[localException name]
    isEqualToString: @"MyException"])
  {
    printf("Meltdown error.\n");
  }

}

NS_ENDHANDLER
{
   printf("In end handler.");
}
return 0;
}
```

Listing 11.10 The main.m program.

```
NS_DURING
{
        .
        .
        .
}
NS_HANDLER
{
  if ([[localException name]
    isEqualToString: @"Exception1"])
  {
        .
        .
        .
  }
  else if ([[localException name]
    isEqualToString: @"Exception2"])
  {
        .
        .
        .
  }
}
NS_ENDHANDLER
        .
        .
        .
}
```

Listing 11.11 Starting main.m.

Handling Multiple Exceptions

You can also check for multiple exceptions. To check for multiple exceptions, you use `if/else if/else` in the `NS_HANDLER` block.

To handle multiple exceptions:

1. Create a file named **main.m**.
2. In main.m, enter the code shown in **Listing 11.11**.

   This code checks for multiple exceptions.

continues on next page

3. Enter the code to add an `else` block (**Listing 11.12**).

   You'll use this block in a later task to pass any uncaught exceptions back up the call stack.

4. Save main.m.

```
NS_DURING
{
        .
        .
        .
}
NS_HANDLER
{
  if ([[localException name]
    isEqualToString: @"Exception1"])
  {
        .
        .
        .
  }
  else if ([[localException name]
    isEqualToString: @"Exception2"])
  {
        .
        .
        .
  }
  else
  {
        .
        .
        .
  }
}
NS_ENDHANDLER
        .
        .
        .
}
```

Listing 11.12 The main.m program.

```
NS_DURING
{
        .
        .
        .
}
NS_HANDLER
{
  if ([[localException name]
    isEqualToString: @"Exception1"])
  {
        .
        .
        .
  }
  else if ([[localException name]
    isEqualToString: @"Exception2"])
  {
        .
        .
        .
  }
  else
  {
        .
        .
        .
  }
}
NS_ENDHANDLER
        .
        .
        .
}
```

Listing 11.13 Starting main.m.

Passing Exceptions Up the Call Stack

Sometimes when you're handling exceptions, you'll want to pass the exceptions back up the call stack to the exception-handling code in a calling function. You can do that simply by raising the exception again in the NS_HANDLER block, as you'll do in this task.

To pass exceptions up the call stack:

1. Create a new file named **main.m**.
2. In main.m, enter the code shown in **Listing 11.13**.

   This code sets up a framework to handle multiple exceptions.

continues on next page

3. Add the code to pass an uncaught exception back up the call stack by raising it again (**Listing 11.14**).

4. Save main.m.

```
NS_DURING
{
        .
        .
        .
}
NS_HANDLER
{
  if ([[localException name]
    isEqualToString: @"Exception1"])
  {
        .
        .
        .
  }
  else if ([[localException name]
    isEqualToString: @"Exception2"])
  {
        .
        .
        .
  }
  else
  {
    [localException raise];
  }
}
NS_ENDHANDLER
        .
        .
        .
}
```

Listing 11.14 The main.m program.

```
NS_DURING
{
        .
        .
        .
}
NS_HANDLER
{
  if ([[localException name]
    isEqualToString: @"Exception1"])
  {
        .
        .
        .
  }
  else if ([[localException name]
    isEqualToString: @"Exception2"])
  {
        .
        .
        .
  }
  else
  {
    [localException raise];
  }
}
NS_ENDHANDLER
        .
        .
        .
}
```

Listing 11.15 Starting main.m.

Returning Values from Exception Handlers

If your exception handler is in a function, you may want to return a value from that function—that is, even if an exception occurs in a function, you may still want to return a value from that function to the calling code. However, you can't just use the return statement in an exception handler—you have to use NS_RETURNVALUE, as you'll see in this task.

To return values from an exception handler:

1. Create a file named **main.m**.
2. In main.m, enter the code shown in **Listing 11.15**.

   This entry sets up exception-handling code for multiple exceptions.

continues on next page

3. Add the code to return values from the exception-handling code (**Listing 11.16**).

4. Save main.m.

```
NS_DURING
{
        .
        .
        .
}
NS_HANDLER
{
  if ([[localException name]
    isEqualToString: @"Exception1"])
  {
    NS_VALUERETURN(0);
  }
  else if ([[localException name]
    isEqualToString: @"Exception2"])
  {
    NS_VALUERETURN(1);
  }
  else
  {
    [localException raise];
  }
}
NS_ENDHANDLER
        .
        .
        .
}
```

Listing 11.16 The main.m program.

```
NS_DURING
{
        .
        .
        .
}
NS_HANDLER
{
  if ([[localException name]
    isEqualToString: @"Exception1"])
  {
        .
        .
        .
  }
  else if ([[localException name]
    isEqualToString: @"Exception2"])
  {
        .
        .
        .
  }
  else
  {
    [localException raise];
  }
}
NS_ENDHANDLER
        .
        .
        .
}
```

Listing 11.17 Starting main.m.

Returning void from an Exception Handler

Exception-handling code in a function can also return a value of `void` from the function (if you want your function to return a value of `void`), but you need a special macro, `NS_VALUERETURNVOID`, to make it do so.

To return a value of void from an exception handler:

1. Create a file named **main.m**.
2. In main.m, enter the code shown in **Listing 11.17**.

   This entry sets up exception-handling code for multiple exceptions.

continues on next page

3. Add the code to return `void` from the exception-handling code (**Listing 11.18**).
4. Save main.m.

```
NS_DURING
{
        .
        .
        .
}
NS_HANDLER
{
  if ([[localException name]
    isEqualToString: @"Exception1"])
  {
    NS_VALUERETURNVOID;
  }
  else if ([[localException name]
    isEqualToString: @"Exception2"])
  {
    NS_VALUERETURNVOID;
  }
  else
  {
    [localException raise];
  }
}
NS_ENDHANDLER
        .
        .
        .
}
```

Listing 11.18 The main.m program.

Catching Uncaught Exceptions

You can set up a special function to catch all unhandled exceptions by calling `NSSetUncaughtExceptionHandler(fn_ptr)`, where `fn_ptr` is a pointer to a function (just like a standard pointer, except that it points to a function) of the form `void NSUncaughtExceptionHandler (NSException *exception)`. So if you don't handle an exception anywhere else, it will be handled in the `NSUncaughtExceptionHandler` function.

To catch uncaught exceptions:

1. Create a file named **main.m**.
2. In main.m, enter the code shown in **Listing 11.19**.

   This code sets up the exception-handling function.

```
int main()
{
  NSSetUncaughtExceptionHandler(
    NSUncaughtExceptionHandler);
        .
        .
        .
}

void NSUncaughtExceptionHandler(NSExceptio
n *exception)
{
        .
        .
        .
}
}
```

Listing 11.19 Starting main.m.

continues on next page

3. Add your exception-handling code (**Listing 11.20**).
4. Save main.m.

   Now your code can catch previously uncaught exceptions.

```
int main()
{
  NSSetUncaughtExceptionHandler(
    NSUncaughtExceptionHandler);
        .
        .
        .
}

void NSUncaughtExceptionHandler(NSException
*exception)
{
  if ([[exception name]
    isEqualToString: @"Exception1"])
  {
        .
        .
        .
  }
  else if ([[exception name]
    isEqualToString: @"Exception2"])
  {
        .
        .
        .
  }
  else
  {
        .
        .
        .
  }
}
```

Listing 11.20 The main.m program.

INDEX

Symbols

A

INDEX

INDEX

I

L

M

N

O

INDEX

INDEX